CHINA

CHINA

The People's Republic of China
and Richard Nixon

Claude A. Buss
STANFORD UNIVERSITY

W. H. FREEMAN AND COMPANY
San Francisco

Library of Congress Cataloging in Publication Data

Buss, Claude Albert.
China: The People's Republic of China and Richard Nixon.

Reprint of the 1972 ed. published by Stanford Alumni
Association, Stanford Calif., in series: The Portable
Stanford.
Bibliography: p.
1. United States—Foreign relations—China. 2. China—
Foreign relations—United States. 3. China. I. Title.
E183.8.C5B87 1974
327.51'073   74-6232
ISBN 0-7167-0771-3
ISBN 0-7167-0770-5 (pbk.)

Printed in the United States of America

1   2   3   4   5   6   7   8   9

Respectfully dedicated

to

three of Stanford University's most
distinguished teachers:

Payson Jackson Treat, the pioneer
of Far Eastern studies at Stanford

Edgar Eugene Robinson, who guided
the History Department with skill and devotion

Graham Stuart, who instilled
the love of diplomacy in the hearts
of many Stanford alumni

This book was published
originally as a part of
The Portable Stanford,
a series of books published by
the Stanford Alumni Association.

CONTENTS

ILLUSTRATIONS

Most of the photographs throughout this volume are from *China—Land of Charm and Beauty*, published by The Shanghai People's Fine Arts Publishing House, 1964. They are identified in that book as follows:

Additional illustrations in this volume:

PREFACE

The People's Republic of China needs to understand the United States and we in the United States have an equally impelling need to understand China. This book is intended as a contribution to that mutual understanding.

In the early days of the Nixon administration, the strained relationship of the cold war pleased neither the People's Republic of China nor the United States. Both nations were ready for cautious steps toward diplomatic normalization. It was paradoxical that Mao Tse-tung, the personification of world revolution, and Richard Nixon, the embodiment of rabid anticommunism, should become the chosen instruments of change from confrontation to negotiation.

The change came more from historical forces within China and within the United States than from the sagacity or will of the respective leaders. Within China, the Communists experienced inevitable difficulties in reconciling traditions and social transformation and in solving domestic problems within the parameters of their ideology. The international sphere challenged the Communists continually to separate friends and foes, to discover policies that would right the wrongs of the past, to lay the foundations for a better future, and yet to satisfy the demands for world revolution. By 1972, Mao Tse-tung and Chou En-lai felt that without abandoning even one of their goals they could with confidence expand their contacts with China's old archenemy, the United States, "the leader of the imperialist camp."

Within the United States, Richard Nixon, as President, indicated his readiness to depart from those political tactics that had stood him in good stead as Congressman, right-wing Republican spokesman, and candidate for the nation's highest political office. He shifted from being a champion of containment to a champion of peaceful coexistence. He clung to his anticommunist principles; he merely modified the methods by which he would deal with the People's Republic of China. Nixon was no longer afraid of the risk he ran in seeking to bring China into what he perceived to be the mainstream of world affairs. He would protect the national interest of the United States in East Asia by trying a new tack.

A certain unreality suffused the unfolding of the diplomatic détente between the former opponents. The meeting at Peking did not reveal the flowering of a beautiful friendship nor the erasure of an unfortunate misunderstanding. It was certainly not a stamp of approval for the possible correctness of each nation's policies nor the harbinger of an entirely new era of tolerance and cooperation. It was but a simple indication on the part of the leaders of both nations that it was better to talk than to fight, and a single step, important in itself, toward the relaxation of tension and reduction of the fear of large-scale war.

In trying to make this study meaningful and also as interesting as possible, my main problem has been to comb through a mass of material and to choose between what should be included and what could be omitted. For the new edition of of this book, I have added an appendix so that the full text of the U.S.-Chinese communiqué, issued at the conclusion of President Nixon's visit to China, could be reprinted.

In putting the material together, I have been as objective as my presumptions allow. My hope is that these pages fulfill even a part of their basic purpose, which is to shed more light on one of the most vital issues in our world today—the relations between the People's Republic of China and the United States.

Stanford, California   *Claude A. Buss*
March 1974

CHINA

中國歷史與共產政策

CHINESE
HISTORY AND
COMMUNIST
POLICY

CHAPTER ONE

CHINESE HISTORY
AND COMMUNIST POLICY

In July 1971, when President Nixon announced his intention to visit Peking, the whole world wondered whether this was a spectacular political gesture or a courageous initiative toward peace for this generation. It seemed to some Americans that the President, having betrayed his principles and deserted his allies, was courting unnecessary danger to national security. To others it looked as if he had taken the blinders from his eyes, cast off the shackles of a disastrous Asian foreign policy, and resumed a dialogue that should never have been discontinued. No one doubted that all humanity would benefit if the United States and China could find a satisfactory basis for peaceful coexistence, and most Americans believed that the risks in the President's gamble were justified by the immensity of the stakes.

The initial effect of the President's announcement was to confirm—perhaps to exacerbate—our prejudices. As individuals, we instinctively approved or disapproved, according to our beliefs, a course of action that seemed to shake the ideological foundations of Richard Nixon's political career. How could he soften up on Communists, whom he had long castigated enthusiastically, and suggest that the time had come for negotiation rather than confrontation? While some critics were accusing him of being hypocritical or mad, others were contending he was only playing politics—using the whole China business as a device to under-cut his dovish opponents in the coming election. Kindlier observers assumed that he was sufficiently flexible to profit from the bitter aspects of recent American experience in Asia, particularly in Vietnam, and to seek victories where he had tasted defeats. Common sense indicated that he had already achieved the highest of his personal ambitions and would, therefore, never launch any new undertaking unless it promised good things for the United States and the world at large. Any President would rather be remembered as a statesman than as a politician.

Sober second thoughts prompted responsible citizens to abandon criticism and strive for understanding. We asked whether the President had really changed his mind about China and Asian Communists in general, and if so, why? Was he ready to admit that the People's Republic of China is here to stay? Could he accept the premise that Peking's point of view on world affairs is entitled to consideration?

We also wanted to know whether, in reviewing the record of U.S.-China relations since 1949, President Nixon had found any evidence that the Chinese are willing to modify their revolutionary hard line and accept a world outlook of live and let live. Would they play down their anti-American propaganda and accept Americans as friends? Was the President willing to concede that perhaps we too have made mistakes, that the Chinese are as suspicious of us as we are of them? Was he clinging to the old concept of China as a menace to noncommunist Asia and a threat to peace, or was he genuinely prepared to seek the normalization of relations on a basis of mutual confidence and mutual respect? In summary, did the Nixon doctrine contain anything genuinely constructive, or was it merely a new formula for the old objective of containing a power regarded as an implacable enemy?

In the confrontation between President Nixon and Chou En-lai, most Americans see a meeting between the chief executive of the most powerful nation on earth and the premier of an underdeveloped country only recently raised up from feudalism. If we are to understand what is happening in the international arena today, we must see more than that. From an historical point of view, President Nixon represents a nation that has no ancient history, while Chou symbolizes a people who are fiercely proud of their ancient cultural heritage and fully aware that the Chinese had invented paper, gunpowder, the magnetic compass, and movable type centuries before the discovery of America.

Although the Communists have dedicated themselves to the creation of a new paradise, they have not turned their backs on three thousand years of history. On the contrary, they vigorously study the past to make it serve present-day political needs. Their scholars are in the process of rewriting history to make it patriotic, popular, and interesting for the masses. They have revised the story of national development to show that the Chinese have always been strong and great. They dismiss inci-

Periods in Chinese History

SHANG DYNASTY
c. 1523 - c. 1028

CHOU
c. 1027-256

CH'IN
221-207
(Great Wall completed c. 220)

EARLIER HAN
202 B.C.-A.D. 9

HSIN
9-23

LATER HAN
25-220

THREE KINGDOMS
220-265
(Period of political disunity)

SIX DYNASTIES
265-589

SUI
590-618

T'ANG
618-906

FIVE DYNASTIES
907-960

NORTHERN SUNG
960-1126

SOUTHERN SUNG
1127-1279

YUAN (MONGOLS)
1260-1368

MING
1368-1644

CH'ING (MANCHUS)
1644-1912

REPUBLIC
1912-1949

PEOPLE'S REPUBLIC
1949-

dents or periods of humiliation as the curse of oppressors and bolster their confidence in the future with the assertion of pride in the past. Because history has become the handmaid of politics, the contemporary policies of Communist China cannot be understood without first considering how the Communists view things in the light of their own experience.

Instead of dividing Chinese history into traditional dynastic periods, communist writers lump everything prior to 1839 into one gigantic category called "premodern." They see the Opium War as the beginning of the modern period, and the May 4 Movement in 1919 as the dividing line between the *old* and the *new* phases of the democratic revolution. In their historiography, the modern period ended and current history began in 1949, when the Communists took over the government in Peking. A review of the vital elements in Chinese traditional history—in our eyes and in theirs—serves the underlying purpose of stressing differences in interpretation that must be ironed out if any progress is to be made toward reconciliation.

China Before 1839

No one disputes that ancient China gave birth to a distinctive culture that ranks with the best devised by human genius. As late as the eighteenth century China contained more books than all the other nations of the world put together. This immense Chinese literary production ranged from poetry to hair-raising tales of adventure. The best of Chinese art, including painting and ceramics, is eternal and universal in its appeal. Chinese craftsmanship is superb—whether in lacquer, bronze, jade, furniture, rugs and carpets, or silk.

The Chinese created a "hundred schools of thought" as rich and varied as a "hundred flowers in a garden." The teachings of Confucius (551-479 B.C.), modified and expanded in myriad ways, dominated the philosophy and political patterns of China down to modern times. Confucianism taught that the foundations of a good society lay in such virtues as human kindness, benevolence, loyalty, and righteousness. Confucius believed in the fundamental goodness of man, the necessity of living in harmony with nature, and the strict observance of form and ceremony in all human relations. He paid precious little attention to the masses, but held that everybody should strive to become superior through learning and right conduct. Other systems of thought and religion flourished side by side with Confucianism and, as a result of their interaction, the people of premodern China were as mature philosophically and as alert intellectually as the Europeans who came to their shores as visitors, merchants, adventurers, or missionaries.

Chinese society, unique in its organization, was headed by the imperial family but dominated by a bureaucracy recruited from the scholar-gentry class. This bureaucracy, about one percent of the population, owed its prestige and position to its learning and its success in passing official examinations in Confucian ideology. The peasants, artisans, merchants, soldiers, and mean people of the villages had no part in the higher life of culture and art.

Because of their self-sufficiency in land, resources, and technology, the Chinese enjoyed a high standard of living and were able to pursue their way of life for centuries in comparative isolation from the rest of the world. To the north lay the cold, barren steppes, to the west the lofty mountains and trackless deserts, and to the south more mountains and steaming jungles. Eternal vigilance was needed on the land frontiers to ward off barbarian invasions. Conquerors like Genghis Khan (1162-1227) soon learned that they could not rule on horseback; they needed the help of Chinese officials and accepted the superiority of Chinese ways and the Chinese language. When Europeans threatened the Chinese in the eighteenth century, they too were regarded as barbarians. Their representatives, received only as tribute-bearers, were expected to kowtow in the traditional manner, three genuflections and nine prostrations before the emperor, who as the Son of Heaven was mediator between heaven and earth. Emperor Ch'ien Lung, "holding sway over the whole world," warned King George III that he was not interested in things strange and foreign and wanted no part of a system of international intercourse implying that any distant monarch could be treated as an equal. China was the Middle Kingdom, the center of the universe, and the British sovereign could do no better than to earn the benevolence of the Son of Heaven.

The Communist Chinese have given some strange twists to such standard accounts by adding theory to the narrative in order to squeeze particularistic Chinese history into the universal Marxian mold. The result is quite a dilemma because they are proud of being Chinese and dislike being equated with any other Marxian example, especially Russia. In 1967, when Mao's Red Guards attacked the "four olds" (old ideas, old habits, old customs, old culture), their primary targets were evil attitudes and apathetic institutions. They exempted such acceptable "olds" as the concept of political unity based on culture, the superiority of the Chinese over other peoples, the pattern of a bureaucratic autocracy, and the key role of military power. These imperialist-communist continuities fit within their polemics and reinforce their claim to a distinctive cultural heritage. Mao left no doubt that he was Chinese and not some kind of a stateless, universal Marxian man.

In retelling their history, the Communists seek to tear down the prestige of the ruling classes and to elevate the heroism of the peasant masses. They prefer the earthy toiler to the superior man of Confucius. In fact, they have attacked Confucius because of his esteem for age over youth, the past over the present, and established authority over innovation. They call him the ideal of the slave-owning classes and the champion of privilege and feudal status quo. As a national monument, unshattered but unworshipped, he is considered valueless as a teacher with relevance to the present. The traditional social order with its ingrained respect for authority, both political and parental, must be destroyed, together with the Confucian philosophy that buttressed it, so that individual freedom can prevail.

Communist historians blast the emperor, his court, the sinister eunuchs, the landlords, and the bureaucracy for political oppression and economic exploitation of the impoverished 80 percent who existed virtually as slaves. The Communists reject the theory of golden ages or dynastic cycles and stress the Marxian laws of social progress. In 1939 Mao said, "The gigantic scale of . . . peasant uprisings and peasant wars in Chinese history is without parallel in the world. These class struggles of the peasants—the peasant uprisings and peasant wars alone—formed the real motive force of historical development in China's feudal society." Mao implies that only ceaseless struggle, and the revolutionary character of the Chinese peasantry as revealed in China's long, dark feudal period, can lead to the inevitable triumph of communism.

Although few non-Marxists are likely to accept this interpretation of premodern China, it is part of the intellectual equipment of every Chinese negotiator, including Chou En-lai. Chinese diplomats also harbor corrosive views about the meaning and significance of the modern period in China's internal development and external relations. In the years 1839-1919 they find all the evidence needed to explain the bitterness they associate with the concept of imperialism.

From 1839 to 1919

By the seventeenth century, Chinese goods, especially tea, silk, and porcelain, were in great demand in Europe. Because there was no corresponding demand for European goods in China, foreign merchants were forced to pay for the Chinese exports with silver. This payments problem continued until the late eighteenth century when Britain discovered that opium grown in India could be sold in China at handsome prices. As the Chinese opium habit increased, the balance of payments was gradually reversed until the Chinese government became alarmed at the drain on silver and banned the import and smoking of opium.

Because the Chinese considered foreign trade a nuisance, they had exacted fees and bribes from Western merchants, still considered barbarians from vassal states, and subjected the traders to capricious rules. Westerners, seething because of the kowtow and determined to pursue their own interests, continued the opium trade at the port of Canton. A battle of arrogance between East and West reached its climax when the Chinese imperial commissioner boarded a merchant vessel and dumped foreign-owned opium worth $10 million into the Canton harbor. The incident precipitated the Opium War between Britain and China in 1839.

When the decayed might of the Manchu empire had fallen before a small British expeditionary force, China was compelled to sign the 1842 Treaty of Nanking, the first of a series of "unequal treaties" through which the West encroached upon Chinese sovereignty. Although the British had done the fighting, the United States—which had bought up the opium supply against the coming war—was happy to share in the profits. The Chinese paid the bill. The merest listing of abuses suffered by China at the hands of the West is sufficient to account for the Communists' emphasis on gunboat diplomacy, imperialism, and the consequent birth of China's permanent revolution.

Under this first treaty, China agreed to open five ports to trade, pay an indemnity, cede Hong Kong to Great Britain to be possessed in perpetuity, and to give up control over its own tariff. Other nations joined in the kill and imposed upon China the system of extraterritoriality by which foreigners and their property were granted immunity from Chinese legal jurisdiction. By the "most favored nation" clause, every privilege China granted to one nation was automatically extended to all.

The Opium War was the first of a series of unequal wars in which Japan and Russia joined the Western nations in scrambling for political and economic advantages in China. Each peace settlement added to China's cup of woe. China lost other territories or claims to territories, including Kowloon, mountain passes in Central Asia, the Amur Valley, the maritime provinces, the Liu Ch'iu Islands (Ryu Kyus), Annam, Sikkim, Burma, Tibet, Macao, Formosa, and Korea. More Chinese ports were opened to foreign trade. Foreigners built their golden ghettoes in major cities along the China coast, in the Yangtze Valley, and in Manchuria. Consulates, banks, clubhouses, warehouses, docks, hotels, Western-style homes, and Christian churches marked the privileged position of the white man in China. The opium trade was legalized. Missionaries were permitted to own land and to travel in the interior. Foreign ships were allowed to dominate the lucrative commerce of the Yangtze and the China coast. It is fair to say that foreigners, with their privileges, were treated better by the Chinese government than were the Chinese themselves. At the same time, coolies were being shanghaied for labor in the United States, and vigilantes in California resorted to jungle law to keep the "wily Orientals" in their place.

China was rendered defenseless both by its military weakness, which the Opium War had exposed, and by its necessary preoccupation with internal strife. The T'ai p'ing rebellion (1850-64) began with a small band of idealistic young revolutionaries, anti-Manchu and antiforeign, demanding reform. It grew to tens of thousands fighting for "a land of great peace" throughout twelve provinces. The biggest revolt in China's

history, it frightened both the ruling elite and the foreigners, who finally helped the Manchus quell the revolution.

In the first years of the T'ung Chih reign, beginning in 1860, men of outstanding talent joined the government and, in their own conservative way, endeavored to restore the glories of traditional Chinese society. They were responsible for the restoration of order and made use of foreign assistance in their modest efforts toward modernization. Although they idealized the past and feared the future, they were powerless to stop the infiltration of Western ideas into China through diplomats, merchants, sailors, missionaries, newspapers, and letters from abroad.

While China struggled with internal problems, Japan put its own house in order and began laying the foundations for an expansionist policy in Asia. Once in control of Formosa and Korea as a result of the "unequal treaties," Japan moved to establish a foothold on the Asian mainland at Port Arthur in Manchuria. The great powers stopped Japan from making that inroad, but their price was high. In return for their assistance, they claimed a series of leased areas, naval bases, and spheres of interest that encompassed every economically or militarily valuable area in China. The Russians established themselves in Manchuria, the French in South China, the Germans in Shantung, and the British in the Yangtze Valley. The Chinese had lost the mastery of their own homes.

In a frantic effort to unify and strengthen the nation, the reform party at the imperial court appealed to the young Emperor, who had just attained his majority and was hoping to wrest power from his regent aunt, the Empress Dowager. During a hundred days in the summer of 1898, the Emperor issued a series of decrees ordering reforms in the government system, in education, in the armed services, and in economic development. The decrees never got beyond the paper stage. When the old dowager learned of them, she ordered the arrest of her nephew and the execution of the reformers.

In the summer of 1900, agitation against foreigners climaxed in the Boxer uprisings. Missionaries were killed and churches were burned. Foreigners were besieged in the British Legation in Peking, and an international expeditionary force, including units from the American 15th Infantry, came to their relief. At the hands of these relief forces, imperial residences were looted and put to the torch, and the court was driven into exile. By the protocol signed when the episode was over, the Chinese were required to pay a substantial indemnity (later returned) and to grant the foreign powers a choice section in the heart of Peking for their legation quarter.

By this time even the rugged old Empress Dowager was forced to concede that the ancient Chinese Empire was near the end of the road. She threw herself into a last-ditch effort to salvage whatever she could through her own reform program, which abolished the official examination system, launched a movement for self-government at the local level, adopted measures to modernize the army and navy, accepted the ideal of mass education, and promised to grant a constitution. When she died before her program was viable, revolution was in the air.

A number of revolutionary groups had joined together to form the Revolutionary League under the leadership of Sun Yat-sen, a Chinese of peasant stock who had acquired a new perspective on China's history while studying medicine at the University of Hong Kong. Sun's platform was based on nationalism (freeing China from foreign control), democracy (overthrow of the Manchu dynasty), and social welfare. The Revolution, which seethed for years before it broke out in 1911, was successful in overthrowing the Manchus and establishing the first Republic of China. The reform movement was aborted, however, when Dr. Sun, in the interest of unity, yielded the presidency to Yuan Shih-k'ai, a warlord who had been commander in chief of the imperial army. Yuan made a few trivial concessions to the reform movement while he continued to make deals with foreign powers and attempted to set up his own dynasty.

The devastating blow to Chinese national pride came at the end of World War I. As one of the allies, China was invited to the Conference of Versailles. When the peace treaty gave the province of Shantung, home of Confucius, to Japan, the Chinese delegates refused to sign the treaty. The delegates returned to a thundering welcome in Peking. For the first time, the Chinese stood up. Students demonstrated, workers went on strike, merchants closed their shops. The outburst of spirit was known as the May 4 Movement (1919), and one who was most caught up in the revolutionary enthusiasm of the time was a former library assistant, then twenty-seven years old, Mao Tse-tung.

China achieved the most influential revolution of the twentieth century under the direction of a former library assistant.

The Communists have no need to embellish China's story from 1839 to 1919 to make it popular, patriotic, and interesting for the masses. They say that the history of this period, which they describe as the Old Democratic Revolution, is a history of imperialist aggression and imperialist opposition to China's development. They charge that foreign imperialist aggressors combined with Chinese feudal oppressors to repress the masses and convert China into a semicolonial, semifeudal country.

In their words, the imperialists helped Chinese feudal power to suppress the idealistic T'ai p'ing revolutionary forces. Then the British invaded southwest China through Burma and the French through Indochina. These ancient dependencies were transformed into foreign colonies, and from these bases the British and French penetrated the South China markets. The British aggressors spread into the Upper Yangtze, established industries along the China coast, and gradually eroded the foundations of China's self-sufficient economy. In further cooperation with the imperialists, the feudalists established an arms industry. Although management was retained by Chinese businessmen, trained by and loyal to the foreign owners, the workers in these factories constituted China's first proletariat. At the end of the nineteenth century, the dominion of monopoly-finance capital gradually established itself. The imperialist powers, no longer satisfied with privileges to dump their goods and plunder the country, now scrambled to acquire leased territories, establish spheres of influence, and place their investments in China.

According to the Communist interpretation, only the long-suffering Chinese people carried on the revolutionary struggle aimed at industrialization and nationalist reform. The Communists distinguish three great waves of revolution: the T'ai p'ing uprising of the 1850s; the social reformers of 1898 and the Boxers; and the revolutionists of 1905-11 who spawned the Chinese Republic. They give a place of honor to Sun Yat-sen for his clear-cut revolutionary stand.

The study of this period produced a profound effect upon the thought and career of Mao Tse-tung. Mao said that he was impressed by the imagery of the communist writer, Lu-hsun, who condemned the twilight of China's great tradition as a "self-serving cover for a cannibal feast." By 1919, Mao said, the main themes in his thoughts were patriotism, resistance to alien rule, self-discipline, self-realization, social responsibility, and the power of the conscious will to influence events. To attain maturity, the Chinese people must replace self-delusion and defeatism with self-respect and self-confidence. A sense of humiliation must give way to a sense of pride. Mao was not satisfied to be a critic; he must be a theorist and a reformer. He was ready for Marxism-Leninism. This was the beginning of personal experience with revolution on the part of the senior Communists who are still in power in Peking. The record of the Chinese nation from 1919 to 1949 is also the story of their lives.

From 1919 to 1949

The transition from warlord control to the foundation of the Nationalist government in Nanking (1928) was marked by the rise of the Kuomintang (the old Revolutionary League reorganized under Dr. Sun

Yat-sen), the birth of the Chinese Communist Party, temporary co-operation between the two, and the emergence of Chiang as the head of the government. Civil wars verged on anarchy, and economic stagnation doomed the masses to a mere subsistence living. China was a country of chaos and poverty when the Japanese invaded Manchuria in 1931.

After Versailles, China's international scene had taken a decided turn for the better. The Western powers showed sympathy for China's aspirations and, at the Washington Conference on Limitation of Armaments and the Far East in 1921, accepted the Nine Power Treaty designed to provide for China the opportunity to develop and maintain for herself a stable and effective government. China was represented abroad by distinguished diplomats and governed at home by officials who made significant progress toward the recovery of lost sovereignty. They demanded the end of unequal treaties, the cancellation of extraterritoriality and tariff control, the abolition of leased areas and spheres of influence, and the departure of such gunboats as the *Sand Pebbles* from Chinese waters. At first the Kuomintang, under the leadership of Chiang K'ai-shek, welcomed the support of the Chinese Communists and took advantage of Russian assistance to strengthen the government, the party, and the army. China recognized Soviet Russia in 1924, but normal relations between the two nations lasted less than three years. The split came in 1927, when the Kuomintang and the Communist Party brought the first united front to an end.

When Chiang came to power in 1928, he undertook policies of unification and modernization. He turned to Great Britain and the United States for major support. He opposed Russia abroad as he fought Communists at home, but his dreams were shattered by the Japanese invasion. Chiang tried to stave off the Japanese by compromising with them, appealing to the League of Nations, and calling upon his allies to take a firm stand against fascist aggression. Chiang K'ai-shek experienced his finest hour in resisting Japan, trading space for time, and scorching the good earth rather than giving it up to the Japanese. While he fought Japan, the disease of the skin, he also fought the Communists, the disease of the heart. He drove the Communists out of their mountain fastness in Kiangsi and forced them to take the Long March, 8,000 circuitous miles to the caves of Yenan in northwest China.

This period of fighting came to a dramatic end at Christmas time, 1936. Hoping to intensify the campaign against the Communists, Chiang flew to the front at Sian, where he was kidnapped by his own generals who hoped to persuade him that it was foolish to waste strength fighting Communists while the invading Japanese were their real and mutual enemy. After a week of arguments in which Communist leaders (among them Chou En-lai) participated, Chiang was released. After this incident, the Communists and the Kuomintang agreed to a second united front; but cooperation existed in name only until the bombing of Pearl Harbor ushered China into a new phase of war, internal politics, and national development.

During World War II one China became three. The China of collaborator Wang Ching-wei, including Peking but with its capital at Nanking, was occupied by Japan. The "Free China" of Chiang K'ai-shek, with its capital at Chungking, bore the brunt of the Japanese attacks. Communist China, with its base at Yenan, carried on guerrilla war against Japan in the countryside. All three claimed to be nationalistic and vowed to end foreign domination in their respective territories. Each one expected to control all of China when the war was over. Occupied China disappeared with the defeat of Japan, but "Free China" battled Communist China for another four long years, 1945 to 1949.

The United States continued to supply Chiang all the forms of aid that had been instituted during World War II when Japan was our mutual enemy. When it became evident, in 1948, that the Kuomintang was losing the civil war, we sent military advisors to help train the Nationalist troops. But word came back from China that, at this point, nothing could save the Chinese from Communism except direct military aid, exercising American authority in China's military operations, and assuming the cost of the China war ourselves. There are still some Americans who blame the United States or "traitors in the State Department" for giving Chiang too little, too late and "selling him down the river." Although it is true that the material aid given to China accomplished little except to prolong the conflict, it is doubtful if any government could have persuaded the American people to take on "somebody else's war" as an epilogue to World War II.

In the view of most Americans, Chiang and the Kuomintang lost the civil war because of their incompetence or corruption. One of Chiang's most obvious failures was his inability to exercise authority over corrupt Kuomintang officials who profited from such practices as extortion, the selling of licenses and privileges, and the mismanagement of foreign relief supplies, and who lived a life of conspicuous extravagance in full view of the poverty-stricken masses. By contrast, the Communist leaders had vowed to eat the food of the masses, share their hardships, and live in the villages on a common level of austerity.

Both the Kuomintang and the Communists understood the importance of solving the problems of land-holding, high rents, exorbitant interest rates, and outmoded agricultural methods. The Nationalist government passed excellent laws dealing with agrarian reform, but failed to implement its program. The Kuomintang had the support of the landlords, the village elders, the bureaucrats, and the local militia. It feared the peasants, who were easily enlisted by the Communist pledge of "land to the tiller."

In the beginning, the Kuomintang had an equal chance to "win the

hearts and minds of the people," but their war-weary armies melted away like snow in the intense heat of the Communists' determination. Instead of becoming dispirited as the fighting dragged on, the Communists shaped the "Common Program," a blueprint for running the government, and never lost confidence in their ultimate victory.

When the Communists relate their version of events between 1919 and 1949, they scarcely recognize the existence of Chiang K'ai-shek and the Kuomintang, but claim for themselves all credit for China's survival, national development, and revolutionary progress. They say, "It was an epoch-making event in China when the Communist Party was born." At the time of its founding (1921) there were only a few dozen members, but they represented a new force, and "new forces are always invincible by nature." They boast, "Nothing could wipe out the Chinese Communist Party, neither the aircraft and guns of the imperialists and the Kuomintang, nor white terror and the tyranny of secret agents, nor the machinations and sabotage of renegades and hidden traitors." On the contrary, during half a century of arduous struggle, it grew into the party leading the People's Republic of China. It was Chairman Mao who built the party, the army, and the united front and adapted the universal truths of Marxism-Leninism to the specific needs of China.

According to the Communists, the New Democratic Revolution (1919-49) went through four historic periods: the First Revolutionary Civil War, the Agrarian Revolutionary War, the War of Resistance against Japan, and the People's War of Liberation. It took all those years to "solve the problem of seizing political power by armed force" and to learn that without armed struggle it would have been impossible for the revolution to triumph. "Political power grows out of the barrel of a gun."

The Communists attribute their victories in the early period to their conviction that whoever won the peasants would win China. Without the poor peasants, there would be no revolution. Mao said, "The peasants are like a tornado or a tempest, a force so extraordinarily swift and violent that no power however great would be able to suppress it." When, in 1927, Chairman Mao himself organized the first contingent of the Workers' and Peasants' Red Army and founded the first rural revolutionary base area in the Chingkang Mountains, he ignited the spark of an armed independent regime. In his struggle to survive against Chiang K'ai-shek, he learned that the seizure of political power by armed force could be accomplished only by setting up rural base areas, encircling the city from the countryside, and finally seizing the cities.

In 1937 when the Chinese revolutionaries entered the war of resistance against Japan, the Communists looked upon the tactic of the united front as "neither all alliance and no struggle nor all struggle and no alliance, but a combination of alliance and struggle." The Communists beat the Kuomintang at the peasant level, by organizing and mobilizing the peasants and moving among them "as fish swimming about in the sea." Mao said, "You can see the difference in our areas [as opposed to the Kuomintang areas]. The people are alive, interested, friendly. They have a human outlet. They are free from deadly repression." During intervals when the fighting slackened, the Communists conducted a rectification campaign within the party to put things in order both ideologically and organizationally. Their objective was "to learn from past mistakes, to avoid future ones, and to cure the sickness to save the patient." By the time of the victory over Japan, the Communists claim, "The army led by our party had grown to a million men, and the liberated areas had expanded to embrace a population of 100 million."

In 1945 it looked, from Asia, as if the power of the United States and its allies was supreme. Refusing to be impressed with this apparent power, the Communists began to develop the doctrine of "the paper tiger." In order to combat the prevailing "morbid fear of the United States," Mao compared the "reactionaries" to the paper tigers and dragons that earlier Chinese armies had carried into battle to startle their enemies. A paper tiger is fierce-looking but impotent. The Communist leaders viewed the United States as a successor to Japan in being the number-one menace to China and regarded Chiang as an American puppet. But they spread confidence that "the paper tiger" would be overcome by the power of the Chinese people.

According to the Communist account, the issue was whether to build a new democratic country for the masses, under the leadership of the proletariat, or a semicolonial, semifeudal country under the dictatorship of the big landlords and the big bourgeoisie. "Our policy was to give Chiang tit for tat and to fight for every inch of land." Chairman Mao pointed out that "giving tit for tat" required a flexible policy. "If they wanted to fight, we would wipe them out completely. . . . If they wanted to negotiate, sometimes not going to negotiations was tit for tat, and sometimes going to negotiations was also tit for tat." In other words, "We fought while we conducted negotiations."

"With revolutionary fearlessness," Chairman Mao had issued the great and timely call, "Overthrow Chiang and liberate all China." Under his leadership "the great Chinese People's Liberation Army wiped out eight million Chiang bandit troops armed by U.S. imperialism, lib-

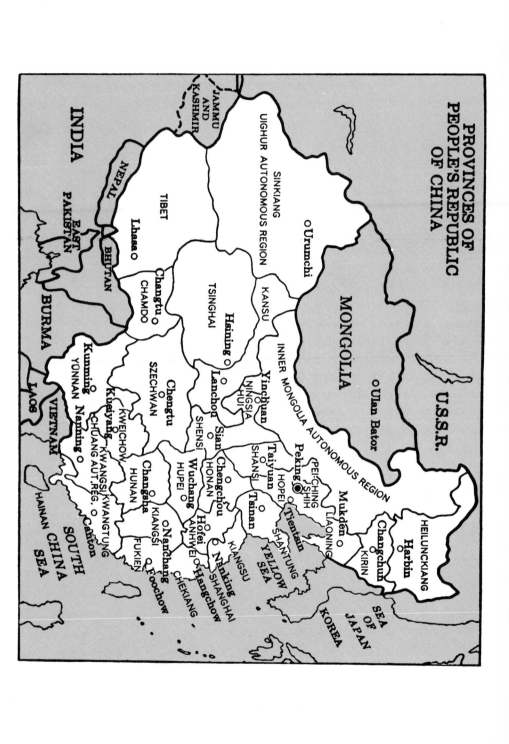

erated all Chinese territory with the exception of Taiwan Province and a number of sea islands, and buried the Chiang dynasty, and the People's Republic of China was founded. The Chinese people stood up."*

By Way of Conclusion

If the Communists accepted our view of history, or were less steeped in their own, the prospects for understanding between the United States and China would be brighter. Guided by their own interpretation of the past, the representatives from Peking are likely to be uncompromising whether negotiating on a bilateral basis or in the United Nations.

The Communists are certain to be tough-minded because they are the heirs of intense and growing nationalism. In the picturesque words of John Fairbank (*Foreign Affairs*, April 1969), "Six decades of change in the nineteenth century and six in the twentieth have destroyed China's inherited order and created an unprecedentedly new one; yet those who see China as broken loose from her old moorings and adrift on the flood of revolution are using an inept metaphor. One can better say the old structure collapsed, its foundations washed out, new plans were imported, and rebuilding is under way, but the site is recognizably the same, the sense of identity [with traditional China] remains. . . . "†

In working for a stronger China, the Communists felt that they were building while they were tearing down. Their deepest commitment was to China and its people. The blood of China is still in their veins, the good earth of China is on their hands. They are still proud of their heritage and will not jettison the past in order to meet the challenge of the modern world. The Chinese leaders are also Communists, but they would have made revolution had Marx and Lenin never lived. The Chinese Communists have no slavish attachment to Russia or to an international communist conspiracy. China is not a satellite of Russia, and Peking's decisions can never be made in Moscow. As the Chinese Communists say, "We have not won our revolution merely to turn our country over to Moscow."

The deference paid to the thought of Chairman Mao will heighten the caution with which Chinese representatives approach any new problem. Every Chinese—for the sake of his own position if for no other reason—wants to live up to the correct line as laid down by Chairman Mao. Sometimes the line is unclear or shifting, and the only security for the man on the spot lies in equivocation or postponement. Decisions with the Chinese will never be made in a hurry.

* All quotes from the official Communist pamphlet, *Commemorate the 50th Anniversary of the Communist Party of China*, Joint Publishing Co., Hong Kong, 1971.
† "China's Foreign Policy in Historical Perspective," by John K. Fairbank, in *Foreign Affairs*, April 1969, Vol. 47, No. 3: 449–463. Copyright 1969, Council on Foreign Relations, Inc. Reprinted by permission.

We cannot discount the role of Chairman Mao in the revolution nor his influence on China's destiny. He is at once a rebel, a visionary, a practical politician, and a capable military leader. He cut off his pigtail (the symbol of Manchu domination) at the age of seventeen. He marched with demonstrating students, became a Communist organizer, fought or cooperated with Chiang K'ai-shek as the occasion demanded. Both Mao and Chou En-lai endured the hardships of the Long March. Mao became the undisputed leader of the party shortly before age forty and has not been challenged successfully in the last thirty-five years. Having fought to reach and stay at the top, Mao once told his younger rivals, "Revolution is not an embroidery party." Many of his comrades have come and gone, and one is never quite sure of the fate of those who have opposed his line.

Although it is possible that fear, force, and terror have been used, Mao's vision of the future and his perception of the correct way to adapt Marxism-Leninism to the needs of China have inspired the loyalty of his followers. He alone is recognized as the arbiter of theory. It is he who has defined the targets, tasks, motive forces, and character of the Chinese revolution. He has been able to surmount crises and catastrophes while concerning himself with the manner in which the world is moving. He demands a proper place for China and for himself in influencing both the direction and the pace of human development. Mao is not a megalomaniac and is not personally responsible for the adulation showered upon him. He knows, however, that as long as his image is useful, it is a device for keeping China united and on target.

We have no way of knowing how much of his thought arose from his own fertile brain and how much has been the product of the elite group with whom he has been associated for so many years. Because he is the heart and head of the organization, whatever is said or written in his name is likely to be accepted as the correct line as long as he lives. His thoughts are written, plainly and intelligently, for all to read. They are more practical than philosophical, yet vague enough to be interpreted in almost any way that expediency requires. For better or worse, Mao has influenced his country and the world as much as any man in his generation. Who will fight for his mantle after his death? How will China get along when there is no longer an accepted authority to pronounce with finality upon the correctness of the line or the nature of heresies on the left or the right? When that happens his memory will be sacred, and until it happens every Chinese representative is likely to strain to do all that Chairman Mao expects of him.

It is evident from the perspective of Chinese history that Americans cannot expect any special consideration from the Chinese because of what we sometimes call our "historic friendship." The Chinese do not blame the American people for the "crimes" committed by the United States government, or for the participation of a small number of American individuals in the "rape of China." They do not single us out for any special condemnation before 1945, but consider us no better than the rest of the imperialist camp, including the British.

Looking over our record, the Chinese place the traders from Boston or Baltimore in the same category with the factors of the English East India Company. We participated in the crime of opium, and the "most favored nation" clause gave us every right and privilege that any other nation enjoyed. Although we did not join with the British or the French in fighting against China, we gave them our help because "blood is thicker than water." After the scramble for concessions at the end of the nineteenth century, we adopted the open door policy and pretended we were China's friends, not because we felt any real love for the Chinese, but because it was the most expedient way to protect our own vital interests. When the United States had reached its own economic maturity, it became the most active of the financial imperialists. After the foundation of the Chinese Republic in 1911, we closed our eyes to the evils of warlordism in order to use the warlord of Peking as an imperialist puppet. We then exposed the insincerity of our commitment to Chinese self-determination when we agreed to turn over Shantung to the Japanese at the Conference of Versailles.

Communist China finds little to praise in the American record between 1919 and 1949. There is no acknowledgement of sympathy for China's nationalistic aspirations nor assistance for China's political and economic development. We promised to help China in the Nine Power Treaty of 1922, but we failed to keep our promises. We hated and resisted the Communists from the beginning and cooperated with Chiang, our ally, only when we could do so on our own terms. The Communists are usually silent on the contributions of the GIs and such Americans as Stilwell, Chennault, and Wedemeyer to the victory over Japan; they point out that we fought Japan, not to help or save China, but to protect the American position in the Far East. When Japan invaded China, we merely proclaimed a spineless policy of nonrecognition and announced some pious principles as tokens of opposition.

The real bitterness between Communist China and the United States began in 1945. According to the Chinese, the American government sent General Marshall to China not to mediate the civil war as we claimed, but only to salvage Chiang K'ai-shek. The formula for a "free, strong, united, and democratic China" was a device to guarantee success for the Kuomintang. The Americans supplied the sinews of war— the weapons, ammunition, airplanes, ships, tanks, trucks, and gasoline used against the Communists—and rejected overtures for peaceful coexistence after the Communist victory.

Against this background, it is easy to see why the Chinese will be as cautious as we, in the effort to restore normal relations.

中華人民共和國的對內政策

**PEOPLE'S
REPUBLIC OF
CHINA:
DOMESTIC
POLICIES**

CHAPTER TWO

PEOPLE'S REPUBLIC OF CHINA: DOMESTIC POLICIES

If the study of the communist heritage indicates that the Chinese will be tough to deal with, the analysis of their record since 1949 leads more forcefully to the same conclusion. Neither historical approach, however, indicates that the American effort to reestablish normal relations with China is hopeless or unreasonable.

The history of China since 1949 is not a mystery or an enigma. The source material is voluminous, the challenge is one of selection and interpretation. Mainland newspapers, magazines, and broadcasts are readily available. True, they are "Chinese propaganda," but they reveal a lot about thought, life, and actual political conditions. Travelers, refugees, and Chinese stationed abroad are usually willing to express their opinions. Universities have an endless variety of courses and institutes dedicated to the study of China and communism. The government, the lecture platforms, radio and TV stations, and the press have their own stables of China watchers. Other lively listening posts include Tokyo, Hong Kong, Singapore, and Delhi in addition to the friendly Western countries that maintain diplomatic relations with Peking and send trade delegations to Canton.

China in 1949 resembled Vietnam today. With their countryside torn by hostilities, the people were war-weary and thoroughly dispirited. They wanted peace and an opportunity to build and were eager for any leadership that promised an end to their suffering. The Communists offered the leadership.

In certain respects, the job of staying in power is different in a totalitarian country than it is in a practicing democracy, and consequently it is more difficult to measure the actual progress that a totalitarian government has made or the degree of success it is entitled to claim. Both systems must find answers to the same questions: how to stay in power, how to feed the people, how to win the hearts and minds of the masses, and how to protect the country from subversion, disunity, or outside aggression. In China there have been no Western-style elections to test the stewardship of the regime. On our side of the Pacific Ocean, there are only incomplete accounts of the intrigues, plots, and tensions that make a mockery of any pretension to unanimity on the part of the men responsible for China's destiny.

China's masses are solid, earthy people with little interest in or knowledge of any ideological theory predating the advent of communism. Because it is not easy to change them, scare them, or force them into a new way of life, the Communist leaders have assumed an enormous task in trying to reshape society and remake the nation. These leaders are mere human beings, with large vision but limited capacity. At best their record is bound to be spotty and zigzag. While they are entitled to credit for much progress, they must also accept the responsibility for setbacks and failures. Chou En-lai told an American visitor in 1960, "Don't ever quote me as saying anything is easy here. Ten years ago all China began a Long March. We have taken the first step—that's all—the first step in a journey of ten thousand miles."

The Chinese leaders are as dedicated to continuing revolution as we are determined that revolution shall not menace our way of life. Whether they have won the masses is open to question, but there is no doubt that they have generated immeasurable strength and power by bringing national politics into every rural commune in order to stimulate the growing national consciousness of 800 million Chinese. It is idle to underestimate the achievements of the Chinese leaders. They have unified China to an extent that it has never been unified before. They have mobilized manpower and womanpower in the service of agriculture and industry to provide strength for the state and jobs for the people. They have made human welfare the first requisite of economic progress; it is not the amount of the wages but the satisfaction of human needs that counts.

In the study of China's domestic policies from 1949 to 1972, the major themes are organization and social control, evolution of the ideological line, economic progress, and human welfare.

From 1949 to 1957

The formation of the People's Republic in 1949 marked the conclusion of the New Democratic Revolution and the beginning of the socialist revolution. Mao Tse-tung was in command and expounded his ideas in a series of pamphlets, chief of which was *On the People's Democratic Dictatorship*. Mao said, "You are quite right, my dear sirs, that is just what we are—a democracy for the people and a dictatorship for the reactionaries." He defined the people as the working class, the peasantry, the urban bourgeoisie, and the national bourgeoisie (merchants and industrialists who had been found acceptable by the Communists). Only the "people" should form the state, choose the government, enjoy freedom of speech and assembly, and possess the right to vote. The "reactionaries," including landlords, the bureaucrat-bourgeoisie, the Kuomintang gang and their lackeys, should be reformed, suppressed, or exterminated. As a temporary expedient, he sought to control capitalists rather than to eliminate them.

Mao wanted to build a strong state apparatus—mainly the army, the police, and the courts—within which he could develop the economy and transform society. Realizing that socialization of the peasants would require a long time, he adopted a land-to-the-tiller policy pending eventual collectivization. He planned an economy balanced between socialized agriculture and a powerful industry having state enterprise as its backbone.

Mao's "Common Program" covered the organs of state power, the military system, economic policy, cultural and educational policy, the status of various nationality groups living in China, and foreign policy. The new government, patterned on the Soviet Union, was headed by a chairman, five vice-chairmen, and a government council. It was little more than an arm of the Communist Party, whose inner circles made appointments and laid down the ideological line. These same individuals controlled the army and the courts. Mao Tse-tung and his intimate comrades wore a variety of hats that enabled them to impose their will on every phase of Chinese life.

When pacification, or "liberation," had been accomplished, the party ranks had to be cleansed of misfits. Every medium of communication became a propaganda tool as the party labored diligently to regiment the masses and erase the remnants of counterrevolutionary ideas. Education and the arts were devoted to socialist goals.

As a prime device for attracting the masses, the Communists passed the Marriage Law of 1950, which placed women on a plane of equality with men. Women have been freed from the crippling effects of foot binding and from the traditional tyranny of the mother-in-law, which once made the Chinese woman little more than a slave in her husband's household. Legally, the Chinese woman has equal rights in matters relating to marriage and divorce and to the ownership of property. Since the state provides child care and expects women to work outside the home, husbands are held equally responsible for housework and child rearing. The Chinese woman is subject to the draft—and she may be working harder than she ever worked before—but her improved status is guaranteed by a law designed to eliminate a long-standing Chinese practice that continued until the Communist regime: Husbands in need of cash can no longer sell their wives and daughters.

Another measure enacted in 1950 was the first nationwide agrarian reform law, which dispossessed the landlords and distributed their goods to the poor. In short order, the Communists cleaned up the wreckage of war, provided food for hungry millions, made jobs whereby city workers could earn a living wage, put a stop to inflation, and launched a grandiose effort for the improvement of industry and trade. All this was accomplished while the Communists negotiated their agreements with the Soviet Union, broke off relations with the United States, and carried on an extensive campaign to "Resist America, Aid Korea, Protect your Homes and Families."

By the time of the Korean War, China exercised a profound influence on the rest of Asia. All Asians, including the 12 million overseas Chinese, identified themselves with the struggle against imperialism and for complete equality in the family of nations. But some Asian leaders (considered reactionary in China) regarded with ambivalence the Chinese struggle between the landless and the landed, the rich and the poor, the privileged and the underprivileged, the bourgeoisie and the proletariat. The Chinese Communists proclaimed themselves the champions of nationalism and revolutionary forces everywhere and used every means at their disposal to demonstrate that Communist China symbolized the wave of the future for all of Asia.

The Korean War was not allowed to interfere with the Communists' task of purifying the party. Chairman Mao launched the "three anti-'s" campaign against corruption, waste, and bureaucratism and the "five evils" campaign against bribery, tax evasion, theft of state property, cheating on government contracts, and stealing of state economic information for private speculation. These campaigns, concurrent with extreme land reform, resulted in compulsory labor, imprisonment, or death for those who were given summary judgments by bamboo courts, those people's tribunals where emotion and hysteria wreaked vengeance in the name of justice.

As in the USSR, the party hierarchy dominated the national government. Nominal power was centralized in a national party congress and delegated to a central committee when the congress was not in session. The central committee elected a secretariat whose politburo was the hard core of leadership. The standing committee of the politburo, headed by Mao Tse-tung, was the ultimate source of authority. Working through committees at every level—regional, provincial, municipal, and district—and acting through the cadres (full-time party workers), the party established its grass roots in cells in every village, township, city block, factory, and school. According to the theory of democratic centralism, information was passed from the bottom up in a democratic manner, and orders were transmitted from the top down to guarantee centralized control. The party line was fashioned at the top. Whatever arguments might exist in secret before the line was formulated, once it was adopted the line became "correct" and could be opposed only at the risk of disgrace—or worse.

The government of China was given permanent form by the Constitution of 1954. The National *People's* Congress (to be distinguished from the National *Party* Congress) was designated as the legislature and the highest organ of state power. By 1964 it had convened only three times. It was scheduled for a fourth session in 1972. Its major function was to choose the chairman and vice-chairman of the government and the Council of State, a kind of super-cabinet. The constitution was the expression of the will of the party, not the product of a popular convention, and could be amended or replaced by the party at will. In effect, the constitution was a facade behind which the interlocking directorate of army, party, and government were guaranteed totalitarian direction of the work of the revolution.

Because of his belief in the necessity of armed struggle and his assumption that political power "grows out of the barrel of a gun," Chairman Mao gave personal attention to the command of the armed forces. The People's Liberation Army, as it was officially called, consisted of 2.5 million men backed by 700,000 in the security forces and 10 million in the militia. After 1955 the PLA was placed on a subscription basis with one young man in ten being drafted at age eighteen. With "a hoe in one hand and a rifle in the other," the PLA was both a fighting force and a working force not entirely set apart from the civilian life of the nation. In addition to being engaged in defense and in farming and small industry, the PLA took part in party work, in education and propaganda, and was looked upon as a political and social force identified with the people. The army was instilled with faith in itself and belief in the perennial danger of invasion.

At the outset, the government attacked the recurrent economic crisis that was aggravated by a terrifying population growth of 15 million per year. In 1953 the government announced the first Five-Year Plan, designed to implement the transition to a socialist society through concentration on heavy industry. Russia agreed to furnish technicians, tools, and machinery, and loans to the extent of $300 million for 156 separate projects. In only three years the government reported the doubling of its industrial production and the increase of industry's share in the national income from 18 to 26 percent. The Chinese renovated old plants, built new ones, improved and expanded the railway system.

In socializing the economy, the government organized small businesses and traditional handicrafts into cooperatives. Small enterprise kept pace with heavy industry in both output and employment. Eighty percent of private commercial and industrial firms were converted into state or joint state-private enterprises. Nine-tenths of all industrial assets passed into the hands of the state as it took control of all foreign trade and most of the internal trade as well.

Because the broader base of land ownership accomplished by the Agrarian Reform Law of 1950 had not brought about a substantial increase in agricultural production, the first Five-Year Plan aimed at increasing the amount of food and raw materials that could be extracted from the countryside. The proportion of investment devoted to agriculture fell far short of that allotted to industry. Irrigation and water control were improved, but little progress was made in scientific seed selection or in the utilization of chemical fertilizers, pesticides, or improved farm machinery. When agricultural production had risen less than 20 percent in five years, peasant discontent pressured the goverment into remedial action.

In another redistribution of land, the poor peasants gained almost a million acres. They were urged to form mutual-aid teams in which seven or eight households combined efforts for peak-season work. Between 1955 and 1957, when about 60 percent of the peasants had entered this arrangement, the mutual-aid teams were consolidated into full-fledged collectives in which the land was owned in common and each member was paid on the basis of workdays contributed.

Signs of unrest and dissatisfaction spread throughout the country in 1956 and surfaced in a dispute between Mao and Liu Shao-ch'i, a veteran party leader and theoretician who had risen to a position of importance in the People's Republic. Liu and his followers argued for a slow-down in the rapid pace of social *transformation*, in direct opposition to the Maoists who argued that time out for social *construction* was equivalent to taking the capitalist road. The cadres became increasingly jealous of the "experts" or technicians, who in turn expressed contempt for the "party hacks." The ideological battle between Liu Shao-ch'i and Mao Tse-tung continued into the second period in the evolution of Peking's domestic policies.

From 1957 to 1965

The problem of uniting the cadres and the intellectuals (coupled with the de-Stalinization campaign going on at the same time in the Soviet Union) prompted Mao Tse-tung to call upon artists and writers to "let a hundred flowers bloom" and upon scientists to "let a hundred schools of thought contend." Mao urged critics among the people to speak out against the regime. For a few weeks both Mao and his skeptical opponents were astounded at the vehemence of the charges against the government, the party, and Mao himself. When the "hundred flowers" had turned to weeds and the free speech movement was threatening to get out of hand, the regime resorted to an antirightist punitive campaign. Those who had followed Mao's urging with too much zeal were subjected to reform through labor, "ideological remolding by physical work."

The second Five-Year Plan for the period 1958-62 was announced in a flurry of optimism with Mao promising "hard work for a few years—happiness for a thousand years" and all of China committed to a Great Leap Forward. Target figures for 1962 would have placed China among the world's leading industrial powers had they been achieved, and for a while it looked as if China had found a magic formula for economic success. But with politics in command, China's economy was wrecked, and the country faced disaster. The Soviet technicians went home. A succession of bad harvests forced China to import food grains. The Great Leap Forward came to an inglorious end in 1961.

The People's Communes, formed in 1957 for the better utilization of rural labor, outlasted the Great Leap Forward. In the commune system all land titles were vested in the communes, which were made responsible for food production, reclamation projects, irrigation and water conservancy, and were also given the mandate to build small factories, machine shops, handicrafts, and cottage industries. They proved their worth, particularly in times of drought and flood. The communes became the key units in party organization and the operating centers for all local government and economic activity. In providing electric power, making tractors available, and teaching mechanical skills to farm hands, the commune became the primary agency for modernization. By 1961 the entire countryside was organized into some 70,000 communes with an average size below 2,000 households, corresponding roughly to a Chinese *hsiang* or township. The direction of population movement in China was from the city to the country.

After the economic disasters of 1959 and 1960, policies of the Chinese leaders shifted significantly. Five-year plans and the Soviet model gave way to traditional Chinese patterns of production and trade. Prime attention was given to agriculture, and light industry was favored over heavy industry. In spite of the taboos of Maoist ideology, the use of material incentives reappeared as the regulations of the communes were modified to satisfy the whims of human nature. The importance of the huge, impersonal commune and its coordination with national policy diminished as emphasis shifted to the functions of brigade and team units and the solution of local problems. Cadres were lectured on the prevalence of bureaucratism and commandism and told to pay more attention to "horny-handed peasants who listen to the wind and sleep with the stars." Each brigade was made responsible for its own labor; a man did not have to go to work in a distant village. Most important, private plots of land were returned to the peasants, who were given free time to work their own gardens and allowed to market their products where prices were best. Although China had to import grain for food throughout the worst years, by 1965 the rural economy was back on its feet.

The recovery of the industrial sector paralleled that of agriculture. Industry produced near capacity by 1963 and achieved a growth rate of 15 percent per year. Technicians and management personnel returned to their posts and displaced the party activists who had taken charge during the Great Leap Forward. In industry as in agriculture, profits once again became the basis of decision making. To speed up production, workers were given bonuses for overfulfillment of quotas and offered piece-rate wages as special inducements. China's industrial progress was indicated by trade fair displays of transistors, computers, television sets, refrigerators, hydraulic presses, diesel locomotives, electronic microscopes, motorcycles, and water-driven turbines.

China repaid in full the development credits extended by the Soviet Union and, by 1965, had repaid all the money it had borrowed. China gave more aid to underdeveloped countries—such as Burma, Cambodia, Nepal, Yemen, and Tanzania—than it had ever received from outside. China's foreign trade ordinarily amounted to less than one-quarter of Japan's. The Chinese exports included high-priced foodstuffs (such as soy beans, rice, frozen vegetables, and processed meats), textiles, paper, and steel. Imports included grain, fertilizer, and industrial goods. In spite of differences in political systems, China enjoyed good markets in Singapore and Japan and traded substantially with Australia, Canada, and Western Europe. After 1965 trade with the noncommunist world exceeded that with the communist nations, and trade with the USSR almost vanished. China imported complete industrial plants from Japan, the Netherlands, and other nations in Western Europe. Tourism and remittances from overseas Chinese brought in more money than China spent on ship charters, insurance, and diplomatic expenditures abroad. China's currency remained stable on foreign-exchange markets, and its international income amount gave evidence of a sound financial condition.

Although this economic prosperity was not great in terms of gross national product and did not keep pace statistically with the spectacular record of Japan, it reflected a basic concern for the welfare of the masses. Agriculture was given priority because so many Chinese depended on rural welfare, and industry was promoted to provide jobs and products for the masses rather than profits for the entrepreneurs. The goals and objectives of economic development in China could not be judged adequately according to Western standards.

It was not clear how much economic recovery was due to Mao's wisdom, his mass line, and how much was due to his rivals who "walked the capitalist road" by compromising with basic ideological tenets. Mao appreciated the progress his peasants enjoyed but resented any dereliction of his teaching. He waged a running ideological battle with his opponents to see that theory and practice would not get too far apart. The dispute was so bitter that in 1959 Mao was obliged to relinquish the chairmanship of the government to Liu Shao-ch'i. Although Mao remained at the helm of the party, his omnipotence had been challenged. With the passing of the economic crisis in 1962, Mao came out swinging for his convictions that the goals of the revolution were more important than immediate economic improvement and that correct ideology was more to be desired than the technology of modernization. To sway public opinion against Liu Shao-ch'i, Mao appealed to Lin Piao, chief of the armed forces, to compile and publish *Quotations from Chairman Mao Tse-tung* (the Red Book), which promoted the mass movement for the living study and application of Mao's ideas. Heroic figures of workers, peasants, and soldiers began to appear on the stage and in works of art. Lin Piao, hailed as the genius who recognized the true value of Mao Tse-tung, was considered Mao's most likely successor.

Mao's campaign for correct thinking worked to stamp out opposition everywhere. Regimentation and social control spread throughout the people's free democratic society.

The party started a socialist education movement designed to stamp out counterrevolutionaries and to correct the thinking of the masses. Mao wanted to obliterate distinctions between the educated and the uneducated, mental and manual labor, the proletariat in the city and the peasants in the country. People's supervisory organs—a euphemistic title for informers and security police—were relied upon for social control. Ordinary citizens in groups of six or more were brought together practically every day to hold discussions or to receive instructions. In these self-criticism meetings, nothing was acceptable except complete compliance with the current party line.

The mass media were required to concentrate on education at the expense of entertainment. More than 60 state-owned publishing houses printed six times as many books and magazines as had the prewar Kuomintang. Chinese periodicals intended for foreign circulation were subjected to rigorous censorship, and the work of foreign reporters was severely limited.

All of China's cultural resources were geared to the creation of proper thoughts—Mao's thoughts—which theoretically would produce right actions. With the Ministry of Culture directing all propaganda activities, the people's participation was achieved through such organizations as the All-China Federation of Literary and Artistic Circles. All talents were devoted to furtherance of the revolution.

With religion under heavy attack as "the opiate of the people," the last of the foreign missionaries were expelled, and Chinese Christians were brainwashed or punished. Christian dogma was reinterpreted as a blend of Christ and Marx. The faithful were exhorted to pray for Marx and Mao and to venerate Christ as the son of a carpenter and a great proletarian leader.

Although the Communists had established an extensive school system dedicated to the training of leaders who would be both "red" and "expert," Mao questioned the value of formal education: "It is not good to read too many books . . . living ideas are better than books. Since ancient times, those who create new ideas have always been young people without much learning. For example, penicillin was invented by a launderer in a dryer's shop, and Benjamin Franklin discovered electricity. Beginning as a newspaperboy, he subsequently became a biographer, politician, and scientist." Mao then said, "Naturally, one can learn something in school. I do not mean to close down the schools. What I mean is that it is not absolutely necessary to go to school."

He expressed these ideas as early as 1958. Six years later he wrote, "The existing system of education won't do. The period of schooling should be shortened. There are too many courses of study at present. They are harmful to people and cause the students to lead a strained life every day." He hated the stereotyped examination system. "Examinations at present are like tackling enemies. They are surprise attacks, full of catch questions and obscure questions . . . I disapprove of them and advocate wholesale transformation." He saw no reason why a student should not communicate with others during an examination or copy from another student's paper. "Furthermore," he said, "students should be allowed to leave the room or to doze off when lessons are badly taught."

The Cultural Revolution, 1965 to 1969

The Cultural Revolution was the general name for everything that happened in China between mid-1965 and the Ninth Party Congress in April 1969. It was a period of civil war without guns, when the ideological controversy between the Maoists and the "top party persons in authority walking the capitalist road" took the nature of a struggle between youth and the party cadres, between revolutionary forces and the old government, between anarchists and the army, between provincial and central authorities, between individual rivals for succession to Mao Tse-tung, and between hard-liners and compromisers on foreign affairs.

In 1965 Mao gave vent to profound disgust with the revolutionary machine he himself had created. He felt that the leaders were growing soft and losing touch with the masses: "The bureaucracy is very busy from morning to night, but they do not examine people. . . . Their bureaucratic manner is immense. They beat their gongs to blaze the way. They cause people to be afraid just by looking at them. They are eight-sided [two-faced] and slippery as eels. Government offices grow bigger and bigger. There are more people than there are jobs. Documents are numerous, instructions proliferate, there is just too much red tape." He set about in deadly earnest to recreate the flaming spirit of the Long March.

Mao encouraged young people to organize themselves into Red Guards and, in a spirit of "doubt everything, overthrow everything," to make a new revolution of their own. In a public crusade against the old traditions, they rooted out all that was left in China of the exotic and mysterious East. They put an end to ancient festivals and to the colorful red wedding and white funeral processions on the city streets. The great Buddhist, Lama, and Taoist temples of Peking were barred, and the Forbidden City was temporarily closed. Red Guards invaded the privacy of homes, destroyed books and art objects, stripped the homes of family altars and ancestral tablets. They stirred up strikes, took over trains, dissolved some communes, robbed state banks, warehouses, and shops. In the name of social revolution, with the thought of Chairman Mao as their guiding genius, rebellious youth reduced the country to turmoil. Mao made no effort to stop them; a little trouble might be a good thing for the country.

In the midst of trouble he formulated a new educational system. On May 7, 1966, he wrote to Lin Piao explaining that he would turn all China into one great school where army men could learn politics as well as military affairs and could engage in agriculture and factory management; where workers and peasants could pursue similar studies; where students and bureaucrats could acquire the skills of peasants and workers. Although the outcome fell short of Mao's grand design, the new approach resulted in "May 7 Schools" in which civil servants, professional men, and backsliding cadres were "re-educated" through a program of manual labor and self-criticism.

Next Mao set up a Central Cultural Revolutionary Group—including his wife, his son-in-law, and three of his most intimate advisors—to take overall charge of the movement. He issued an order to drag out all the counterrevolutionary, revisionist bourgeoisie still nestling in the party, the government, and the army. He closed the schools and told the students to join the Red Guards. A year of chaos ensued. Anyone could bring charges against anyone. Some of China's most distinguished civil and military leaders were dismissed in disgrace, while artists and professors were dunce-capped and paraded as bourgeoisie through jeering mobs. Conservatives in the party leadership were horrified at the excesses of "ultraleftism," which resulted in a near-mutiny on the part of military regional commanders in July 1967, an attack on the British Embassy, and the occupation of the Foreign Ministry by revolutionary rebels during the following month.

Chaos led to a fundamental reassessment of the revolution. Mao seemed to be out of favor with everyone. Conservatives held him responsible for undermining the institutions of the party and the army and, according to rumor, plotted to assassinate him. Ultraleftists accused him of losing his nerve in failing to follow through with his own extremist convictions. Mao confessed that he had not foreseen that the whole country would go into uproar, and it is possible that he himself called for sanity. It is equally possible that Mao's opponents curbed the Red Guard against his will. After restrictions were placed on the Red Guards, they descended to factional fighting, and army units restored order throughout the country. Violence was condemned. Students and workers were ordered back to their normal pursuits as the revolution simmered down to a sustained verbal attack on Liu Shao-ch'i.

Mao's objective was not merely to defame his old comrade in arms, but to uproot his ideas and influence. Liu's revisionist line, attractive to millions, had gained organizational support within the party, the government, and the army. Knowing this, Mao chose to expose Liu and his followers thoroughly before cleaning out the clique and to temper the masses in the bitterness of class struggle. In 1968 Liu was deprived of all his posts and more of his followers were purged.

The ideological battle left its scars on every member of China's leadership. Confidence in the old party-government setup was shattered. The army kept order while the administrative system was refurbished. Revolutionary committees, representing the army, the reformed cadres, and the masses of old, middle-aged, and young people, were organized to replace the old party committees at every level from the cells to the provinces. The Communists claim these committees "emerged from the victory in the proletarian revolution and gave our party and our country more vitality than ever." The Ninth Congress of the party was called

---

**Seeds of anarchism and factionalism were still alive . . .
China seemed impossible to rule from
a single desk in Peking.**

---

in April 1969 "to consolidate the victory," as they phrased it, to adopt a new constitution for the party, and to reconstruct the high command under Mao Tse-tung and Lin Piao. The party promised a new People's Congress as soon as the organizational work could be performed and preparations made for the necessary elections; but as differences in the high command came more and more into the open, the organizational work became more difficult to accomplish, and the new People's Congress was repeatedly delayed.

Since the Cultural Revolution

When the Cultural Revolution was formally ended, no one could be sure who won. On the surface it looked as if the Maoists won, yet the giant posters of Mao came down, the Mao buttons shrank in size, and his garishly-painted slogans were allowed to fade. It was hard to say whether Mao's policies had carried the day or to imagine that those who had enjoyed prestige and power for two decades could remain silent or inactive after their ouster. Tension would not disappear overnight. It was by no means certain that Mao, in tearing down the scaffolding by which he had climbed to power, had produced a viable substitute.

The Communists said, "Chairman Mao teaches us that no one must think that everything will be all right after one or two great cultural revolutions, or even after three or four." They knew that seeds of anarchism and factionalism were still alive and expected protracted struggle against bourgeois revisionism as long as the thought of Liu Shao-ch'i lingered. Antagonisms persisted between age groups and interest groups and against leadership of the army, industry, schools, and urban areas. Leaders in the localities were distrustful of the central authority. China was not likely to break down into sovereign states, but the central government might never recoup the power over the provinces that it had enjoyed in the 1950s. Recovery of self-confidence and stability strengthened the instinct for autonomy at every level—household, village, county, province, and region—and made China progressively more difficult to rule from a single desk in Peking. While the Communists claimed that the Cultural Revolution was a glorious success, the outsider wondered whether Mao was asking too much of human nature. Could he really change the patterns of human thought and behavior and make the ideal of social service more appealing than the incentive of individual betterment?

Whatever success Mao may have attained in inculcating his ideology, he did not find the elusive clues to the solution of economic and social problems. He had put forth an empty argument, that indoctrination was more important than technical factors in bringing about modernization. Wanting desperately to produce a Great Leap Forward, Mao could not find the formula. He introduced a third Five-Year Plan in 1966 but quickly abandoned it. It is possible that only the skill of the administrators saved China from economic disaster after the chaos of the Cultural Revolution. The vague principles of the "reds" must have been the despair of the "experts" who needed to harvest the crops, run the trains, and balance the budget.

The Cultural Revolution did not provide the answer to the question of Mao's successor. For a time it looked as if Lin Piao and the army had emerged in an unassailable position, since the army dominated revolutionary committees and ran most of the schools, factories, and communes in the country. But as an individual, Lin Piao had his rivals, including regional generals who challenged the central command. Professional soldiers on the general staff were concerned about the inferiority of China's weaponry and recognized the value of possible foreign (Russian?) assistance. The party, on the other hand, was determined to enforce Mao's principle: The party controls the gun.

It would be a mistake to limit this discussion of China's internal affairs to the parades, the propaganda posters, and the little red book. The ideological controversies of the leaders reveal less of the heart and soul of China than the welfare, dreams, and goals of its countless millions. The place of Mao Tse-tung and his comrades in China's history will be determined by what they have done for the people, rather than by the theories they have conjured up.

It may take China a half-century to reach the point in economic development that the richer nations of Western Europe now enjoy. China has 25 percent of the world's people and only 4 percent of its wealth. (By contrast, the United States has 6 percent of its population and 35 percent of its wealth.) China is poor and its economic prospects are bleak. The average income of a worker is about $20 a month, of which $6 is spent for food, $2 for housing, and $2 for clothes. Transportation and medical expenses are practically free, and no one pays income tax because the state gets its money from agriculture and state-owned enterprises. In spite of their Spartan way of life, the Chinese masses have a better standard of living than they have ever known in the past. Families are able to save enough to purchase such status symbols as bicycles, wrist watches, sewing machines, and radios. A bicycle costs about three months' wages.

The Chinese are making progress with some of their radical social innovations, such as the communes and their subdivisions. The prestigious University of Peking has become an educational guinea pig. Requirements for admission, in addition to high school education and physical fitness, include advanced ideological preparation, ability to study Mao's thought "in a living way," and willingness to serve the people wholeheartedly. Teachers and students are required to learn together and to integrate their learning with agricultural production, industrial production, or military affairs; the schedule is divided between part-time schooling and part-time work. Chinese research in applied science, practical medicine, and acupuncture has made spectacular headlines.

Less edgy than Americans, the Chinese
are a nation of young people—poised, confident,
ready to move mountains with a teaspoon.

According to eyewitness accounts by recent travelers, the Chinese people are cheerful, poised, courteous, and self-confident. China impresses outsiders as "a nation of young people—ambitious, zestful, energetic, and enthusiastic—controlled by a government run by the very old." In spirit, it is a different world from the United States. Described in terms of regimentation, discipline, austerity, China has been called "a sink of Puritan morality." And yet, in comparison to Americans, the Chinese appear less edgy, more at ease with themselves, pursuing their lives in a relatively unpressured way. The Cultural Revolution, apparently, has impressed the Chinese less than it has impressed the China watchers. It has taken its place as "a step in a long journey" in the hearts and minds of the ordinary people. Although they are concerned with class-struggle, since it is continuously hammered into them, they are also worried about mother's health, boiled rice, or an evening at the people's ballet. There is no such thing as freedom as we know it, but today the people are controlled by politics and persuasion rather than by terror.

Courtesy is still prized and practiced, although its greatest philosopher has been repudiated. China is a huge world of its own, with its old-fashioned patience and politeness, where the principal content of daily life is the proper conduct of encounters with neighbors, friends, visitors, and officials. The Chinese believe in themselves. They do not take kindly to any capitalist who would presume to point out the error of their communist ways. They are aware that China has stood up, that class exploitation is gone; and although the nation is now proletarianized, it is on its way to something better. Like the old man in an ancient Chinese fable, they can "move mountains with a teaspoon." Naturally, Chairman Mao has interpreted the fable to fit the China of today: The "mountains" that must be moved are feudalism and imperialism.

中華人民共和國的外交事務

PEOPLE'S
REPUBLIC OF
CHINA:
FOREIGN
AFFAIRS

CHAPTER THREE

PEOPLE'S REPUBLIC OF CHINA: FOREIGN AFFAIRS

> Over the past twenty years and more, it is not we who have caused harm to others, but the U.S. government which has been causing harm to other countries and other peoples.
>
> Premier Chou En-lai to Mr. James Reston,
> Peking, August 9, 1971

Americans see Communist China's role in international affairs as that of a "militant, dynamic, ruthless, aggressive, expansionist" power dedicated to the destruction of imperialism and, ultimately, to domination of the world. Conversely, the Chinese see the American commitment to peace in Asia and the rights of small nations as the crassest kind of aggression and a veiled threat to China's national existence. The most difficult aspect of seeking better Chinese-American relations will be the modification of these attitudes of distrust. Each must respect the integrity of the other nation's motivation in international relations.

Although Mao has paid almost as much attention to the completion of world revolution as he has paid to his other goal, the achievement of a communist society at home, there is more rhetoric and less precision in his statements about the world revolution, which suggests that foreign affairs are less vital to him than domestic policies. The fate of the communist regime and the outcome of the struggle for party leadership will be determined by circumstances within China, not by the vicissitudes of external relations. China's future depends upon the welfare of its own peasants, not upon the goodwill of the United States or Russia or the strength of Chinese fighting forces.

Communist China believes that there will be war as long as capitalist imperialism exists, that armed struggle must be the central, unavoidable process of revolution because the imperialists will never surrender without a fight. In order to bury capitalist imperialism, the Communists must first destroy it. In Peking's view, China has become the champion of the working classes and oppressed people everywhere, and must give its support to all wars of liberation. This does not mean that China will start insurgency movements or fight other people's battles. China holds that revolution is not for export and, as Chou En-lai told Nasser, each struggling people must learn to stand on its own two feet. China will do no more than extend help and encouragement.

The People's Republic has professed a special interest in overseas Chinese who were overlooked or neglected by Peking for many years, particularly the Chinese in Southwest Asia, who enjoy economic power that could conceivably be turned to political advantage. Peking understands that most overseas Chinese are capitalist to the core, hard-working and ambitious, without any affinity for socialism or communism. Furthermore, they are suspect in the nationalistic-minded countries in which they live. But they are Chinese in blood and "Once a Chinese, always a Chinese." Peking has invited overseas Chinese to visit the mainland almost at will and has given special privileges to their relatives in China.

Whatever clandestine measures might have been taken involving overseas Chinese on party or individual levels, official government attitudes and pronouncements from Peking have been circumspect. Peking has urged its people overseas to respect the laws and customs of the countries in which they live, to stay out of local politics, to invest their capital in local industries, and to send their children to local schools. Peking wanted them to come to terms with local nationalism without breaking their ancestral ties. While giving assurance to the various countries involved that overseas Chinese would not be used for subversive purposes, Peking has made public statements that it would protect the legal rights and interests of all Chinese living abroad, that it would not tolerate "any injustice or insult to our fellow countrymen on foreign soil"—which ostensibly includes the United States as well as Southeast Asia.

The heart of China is in Asia, and it is in terms of Asia that China's vital interests must be adjudged. Communist China's determination to assert its influence (not necessarily to make itself predominant) in the Asian region follows the classic pattern set by strong dynasties in the

past. China looks at Asia as we look at the Americas. Because security of the home base is essential, minority problems must be subordinated to security, and potential enemies must be kept as far away as possible. When a threat appears, every risk is acceptable in order to meet the challenge. Since China's home base includes Tibet and Taiwan, the effort to implement Chinese sovereignty in these areas—in Peking's view —cannot possibly come under the heading of international aggression. Manchuria, Inner Mongolia, and Sinkiang are likewise deemed to belong exclusively to China's sovereign domain.

China's problems in its own inner Asian areas are of two kinds: relations with indigenous peoples and the possibility of conflicts with foreign powers. In Manchuria the first objective is to guarantee the security of this rich land from any possible external menace. Communist China is very alert to the dangers to Manchuria inherent in the Russian economic development of Siberia and in the possibilities of future Russian-Japanese technical collaboration. The recently-opened Moscow-Tokyo air route passes just north of Manchuria. The Chinese are also aware of the Russian military build-up along the Manchurian frontier. Furthermore, the Chinese feel that the northern watershed of the Amur River and the maritime provinces rightfully should be restored to China.

Racial animosities are more significant in Mongolia than in Manchuria. The Mongols are divided into the Russian-oriented Mongolian People's Republic (Outer Mongolia) and the Chinese Inner Mongolian Autonomous Region. In Outer Mongolia, which is nominally independent, the Chinese have lost out in their effort to counter the influence of the Soviet Union. The historic animosity of the Mongol race toward the Chinese complicates China's endeavors to minimize ordinary administrative problems and further economic development in the Inner Mongolian Autonomous Region. The Chinese atomic bomb testing site is in Inner Mongolia.

In Chinese Turkestan, or Sinkiang, the Peking government has taken care to see that the different ethnic groups—such as Kazak, Uzbek, and Kirghiz—do not try to unite with their kinfolk in Soviet Turkestan to form a single Turkic nation. China has established firm political control in Sinkiang and has effectively displaced Russian influence. Peking has also undertaken economic development and immigration programs intended to bind Sinkiang closer to China proper. Communist China has accused the Soviet Union of stirring up trouble on the China side of the border and of carrying out provocative military maneuvers unreasonably close to Chinese territory.

Tibet has been Communist China's most difficult minority problem. The Tibetan way of life emphasized the Buddhist religion, the Dalai Lama, and a feudalistic hierarchy of nobles and monks. China occupies Tibet with a large military garrison and relies on force to prevent an explosion of Tibetan nationalism. Peking has carried out an intensive policy of Sinification and has built strategic motor roads between Lhasa and western China. Although Peking considers Tibet exclusively a Chinese problem, China's Tibetan policy has caused bitter relations between China and India, produced significant agitation at the United Nations, and aroused sympathetic world opinion on behalf of the Dalai Lama.

Since the war with India in 1962, the Russian borders on the north and west represent China's only territorial danger spots. China has shown restraint with regard to Hong Kong and Macao but has let it be known that nine unequal treaties, including three with Russia, will have to be settled. Because China wants friendly neighbors, it cannot be too energetic or too aggressive for fear of generating counterpressures or stirring up age-old antagonisms. Preferring prestige to political control, Peking employs every artifice of carrot and stick to exert what it considers to be the optimum influence. China conducts trade programs for political benefit, openly extends aid and support in such "wars of liberation" as those in Vietnam, Cambodia, and Laos, and presumably helps insurgents in Thailand and Burma. China may even send "volunteers" as in the case of Korea.

Looking beyond China's immediate neighbors, it is impossible to confirm that China seeks sources of raw materials or markets to control or territories to dominate. China has no great-power alliances except the shaky one with the Soviet Union and has shown no disposition to participate in any great-power combination or alliance system, even against the United States. As security aims, China seeks to drive American military power out of the western Pacific and Southeast Asia, reduce the Russian menace on the frontiers of inner Asia, prevent the rise and expansion of Japanese militarism, and make itself, not Russia, the inspirational center for the revolutionary peoples of the world. By accepting membership in the United Nations, China has indicated a desire to assume its rightful place in the world community and have its say in fixing the rules and standards by which international relations should be conducted in the modern world. In discussing the normalization of U.S.–China relations with President Nixon, neither Mao Tse-tung, Chou En-lai, nor any other Chinese leader sees any need to apologize for China's diplomatic record since 1949.

In discussion of China's foreign affairs, the spotlight shifts from Mao to Chou En-lai, who became premier and foreign secretary in 1949, after thirty years of arduous labor on behalf of Chinese Communism, and has since earned an international reputation as a suave and gracious negotiator. Hard-working, dedicated, Chou En-lai possesses the qualities that would have made him a leader regardless of his time or place, but has not demonstrated a Napoleonic lust for personal power. Chou has been a complement, rather than a rival, to Mao Tse-tung. It is Chou, the organizer, who transcribes Mao's ideology into operating procedures by building new institutions, giving new form to old institutions, devoting his attention to big movements without losing sight of details. Chou, who can deal effectively with the intellectual elite or with hard-headed radical insurgents, is credited with success in rallying competitive political factions into a unified movement behind the Peking regime.

Foreign Affairs from 1949 to 1954

When the Chinese Communists came to power, they based their foreign policies on a "Common Program" to protect China's independence, freedom, and integrity; to work for lasting peace and friendly cooperation among all countries; to unite with the USSR and all communist states against the camp of the imperialists headed by the United States; to protect the overseas Chinese; and to establish diplomatic relations with any foreign governments that severed relations with the Kuomintang and adopted a friendly attitude toward Peking.

Flushed with victory in the civil war, the Chinese wanted most of all to complete the consolidation of China by the conquest of Taiwan. In this ambition they were thwarted first by their own weakness and subsequently by the opposition of the United States. In 1950 the Chinese marched into Tibet and promised the quick establishment of an autonomous region. They were in no position to improve their stature in Southeast Asia and undoubtedly hurt themselves by adopting an unsympathetic posture toward the "neutrals" in the cold war. Nehru tried to be friendly, but the Chinese merely referred to him as a "sham" and an "imperialist lackey." China called Pakistan a puppet of the capitalist world and warned the leaders of Burma, Cambodia, Indonesia, and Laos that they would have to "lean to one side." They were told there was no middle road; the neutrals would have to declare for the Communists or be considered against them. China recognized Ho Chi Minh as the president of all Vietnam, gave Ho as much help as possible against the French, and supported him during and after the Geneva Conference.

The Chinese signed economic agreements and a treaty of alliance with Russia on February 14, 1950. The Russians were allowed to participate in the economic development of Manchuria and Sinkiang and were permitted the joint use with China of the Port Arthur naval base. Russia and China agreed to mutual assistance in the event that either was attacked by Japan or a power in concert with Japan (clearly a reference to the United States, which was then in charge of the Japanese occupation). Russia, China, and North Korea presented a solid front against the forces of the United Nations during the fighting in Korea and the negotiations that followed. As long as Stalin lived, he was Russia to the Chinese Communists. It was he who extended recognition, signed the treaty of alliance, provided the sinews of war, granted economic

THE PEOPLE'S REPUBLIC OF CHINA SINCE 1949

DOMESTIC POLICIES		FOREIGN AFFAIRS
Establishment of People's Republic of China	1949	Common Program, Aid to Viet Minh, Break with U.S.
Agrarian Reform Law	1950	Alliance with U.S.S.R. Korean War
Marriage Law and Party purification movements	1952	Government of the Republic of China (Taiwan) treaty with Japan
First Five-Year Plan	1953	Reliance on aid from U.S.S.R.
First National People's Congress adopted Constitution	1954	Khrushchev and Bulganin visit China Geneva Conference—Peaceful Coexistence
	1955	Talks with U.S. at Geneva begin
Eighth National Party Congress	1956	Chou En-lai goodwill trip to Southeast Asia
Hundred Flowers Campaign	1957	Ideological split begins, U.S.S.R. Afro-Asian Conference
Liu Shao-ch'i replaces Mao as Chairman Communes established Second Five-Year Plan Second National People's Conference Beginning of Great Leap Forward	1958	Talks with U.S. shift to Warsaw Offshore Island crisis with U.S. (Quemoy, Matsu)
Lin Piao placed in command of People's Liberation Army	1959	Troubles with India and Tibet
Second of four bad harvests	1960	Series of border agreements (India, Burma) Russian technicians leave China
New Socialist Education Campaign	1962	Geneva agreement on Laos Border war with India
	1963	Second Afro-Asian Conference Failure of Soviet-China talks on ideology
Third National People's Congress First atomic explosion	1964	Chou En-lai tour of Africa Recognition by DeGaulle's France U.S.S.R. arguments: Sinkiang, Amur Gulf of Tonkin incident
Cultural Revolution begins Lin Piao article on world revolution	1965	Support for northeast Thai insurgents Sides with Pakistan in Kashmir
Year of chaos	1966	
Climax of disorder	1967	Nadir of international prestige in West
Restriction of Cultural Revolution	1968	Diplomatic fence mending
Ninth Party Congress End of Cultural Revolution	1969	Border talks with U.S.S.R. begin in Peking
	1970	Sanctuary to Sihanouk of Laos Recognition by Canada, Italy
Party reorganization New leadership struggles	1971	Nixon visit is announced Admission to U.N. Backs Pakistan in India war

aid, and prevented ideological differences from coming to an open break. Stalin treated China as a partner—a junior partner but not a satellite—and when Stalin was buried, Chou En-lai marched with distinguished Russian leaders in the funeral procession.

Between 1949 and 1954 Russia was China's number-one friend and the United States was China's number-one enemy. In Chinese pronouncements, the United States succeeded Japan as the militarist, fascist aggressor in East Asia. General Marshall was labeled, not a genuine mediator in the civil war, but the undisguised backer of Chiang K'ai-shek. He was blamed for turning over guns and equipment to the Nationalists, moving their troops, and making possible the Nationalist blockade of Communist ports and supply lines. The United States was condemned for continuing its recognition of the government of the Republic of China on Taiwan and depriving mainland China of its right to China's seat in the United Nations. China went to war against us in Korea and opposed us in Vietnam, where we recognized Bao Dai and Communist China recognized Ho Chi Minh.

The sense of direct threat to China's territory played a major part in China's decision to send its volunteers across the Yalu River late in 1950. China did not seem eager to rescue Kim Il-sung, the leader of North Korea, or to enter the fight to share Russia's burdens. But the Chinese came into the war, as they said they would, when the Americans and our allies crossed the 38th parallel. Chou En-lai told James Reston in 1971, "It was you who occupied Taiwan and the Taiwan Straits. You pressed on to the Yalu. We could not stand idly by. It was the United States who committed aggression against China, not vice versa."

The Korean War was only the beginning of the confrontation with the United States. Chinese anger mounted as the Americans built up the military potential of Taiwan, increased military assistance to the French in Indochina, and accelerated a program of technical, economic, and military assistance to the nations of Southeast Asia. The American goal under President Truman, and under his successor, President Eisenhower, was clearly the containment of communism and Communist China.

During this period nothing frustrated the Chinese more than their relations with Japan. For fifteen years Communists and Nationalists had shared the suffering of the nation at the hands of Japan. Yet Communist China was not permitted to share in the victory celebration, to participate in the occupation of Japan, or to plan jointly for China's protection in the face of a reviving, pulsating Japanese nation. Inevitably, China thought in terms of reparations from Japan; the Japanese should have to pay for the immense, unspeakable wrongs they had inflicted upon China before peace could be restored in East Asia. From the moment the occupation of Japan was undertaken, China was faced with the reality that the United States was dedicated to "helping Japan up, not keeping Japan down." The image of General MacArthur was not a pleasant one in Communist China.

China's treaty with Russia, against Japan or a power in concert with Japan, took on additional significance when China had entered the Korean War and had perceived the extent to which the success of United Nations troops was due to the friendly cooperation of Japan. The United States and Japan were factual allies, and Japanese territory was the main staging area for the war effort in Korea. The 1951 peace treaty between Japan and most of its former enemies caused further consternation in Peking, where it was termed a war treaty rather than a peace treaty because the rights of Communist China were disregarded. The subsequent treaty (1952) between Japan and Chiang K'ai-shek's China was labeled by the Peking government "an open insult and an act of hostility to the Chinese people."

China then began a desperate campaign to draw a line between the interests of the Japanese people and the acts of the "reactionary" government. On the eve of Japan's newly regained independence, China begged Japan to liberate itself from the United States. As gestures of goodwill, Peking launched sympathetic propaganda campaigns addressed to the Japanese people, proposed expansion of trade relations and cultural exchanges, and facilitated the return to Japan of the last of the Japanese residents in China who wanted to go home. This desire to improve relations with Japan was one of the major factors inducing China to pursue a new direction in foreign policy beginning in 1954.

From 1954 to 1957

For a short span of three years China departed from its hard line on world revolution and followed the soft line of peaceful coexistence. These years, 1954-57, which looked like years of domestic stabilization and prosperity, turned out to be the incubation period for "walking the capitalist road." The evidence is inconclusive with regard to Mao's stance on foreign policy during this period. While he opposed the willingness of his colleagues to stray from austerity in the revolution at home, did he also oppose the inclination to compromise with sworn ideological enemies abroad? Or did he then—and does he now—perceive a national advantage in using foreigners to work for China?

Until 1954 Peking had talked of liberating Taiwan by force, but was silenced by the American build-up on Taiwan, the American treaty with Chiang K'ai-shek, and the Formosa Resolution, which in certain contingencies authorized the use of American forces for the protection of the offshore islands. Then in 1955 Chou En-lai began making overtures to the West to negotiate on behalf of peaceful coexistence. These offers were declined by the United States.

At the Bandung Conference of African and Asian states in April 1955, Chou En-lai made a public offer to sit down and enter into negotiations with the United States to discuss the question of relaxing tension in the Far East, particularly in the Taiwan area. He also indicated that he was willing to negotiate with local authorities on Taiwan for the peaceful liberation of the island. The Chinese tried to persuade Taiwan to turn against the United States and even went so far as to offer Chiang K'ai-shek a high post in Taiwan under the Peking regime.

In the border areas, China persuaded Russia to return its economic privileges in Manchuria and Sinkiang. China had no assets to enter into a contest with Russia in assisting in the economic development of Mongolia, but it set up the Sinkiang-Uighur autonomous region in 1955 to consolidate its western frontier. China took firm action in Tibet with a massive military occupation and sought to placate India by negotiating the first of a series of treaties based on Chou's five principles of coexistence. Chou declared that China would negotiate with any nation (including the United States) a treaty based on the principles of guarantee of territorial integrity, nonaggression, noninterference in internal affairs, equality and mutual benefit, and peaceful coexistence.

Following the 1954 Geneva Conference—which was convened to deal with the problems of Korea and Vietnam—Chou launched a determined campaign to reduce the influence of the West and to improve China's position in South and Southeast Asia. China exchanged recognition with India, Pakistan, Ceylon, Nepal, Indonesia, Burma, and Cambodia. Instead of continuing opposition to "neutralism" on an ideological basis, China courted the neutrals. The new formula was, "As long as you are against imperialism, you are with us." China solicited the cooperation of the neutrals on the basis of mutual national interests: anticolonialism, Asian solidarity, race consciousness, love of peace, disappointment with Western-style democracy, and determination to end poverty. Chinese officials paid visits of state to the neutralists, and presidents, princes, and prime ministers returned the calls to Peking. At the same time, China reduced the clandestine help that had gone to the support of communist insurgents in neighboring countries.

In three short years, China achieved substantial results with its peaceful coexistence line. China cemented its solidarity with North Vietnam; established common understanding with India, Pakistan, and Nepal; and reduced the fear and suspicion that had accumulated in such unsympathetic countries as Thailand, Malaya, and the Philippines. Under Chou's five principles, China and Burma signed a series of agreements that led to the establishment of consulates, the opening of air and highway communications, peaceable settlement of border problems, and movement toward a dual nationality treaty. China promised to buy Burmese rice and to stop aiding communist rebels in exchange for Burma's promise to prevent its territory from being used as a base for hostile military operations against China.

The amiable Chou En-lai received his warmest response from Sukarno, the extrovert president of Indonesia. Chou promised Sukarno unqualified support against rebel factions in Indonesia, including the Communists, and against the Dutch, who clung to their unpopular claim to West Irian. In 1955 Chou and Sukarno negotiated a treaty on dual nationality. Chou was equally ingratiating and successful in concluding a working arrangement with Prince Sihanouk of Cambodia.

Chinese skills were most severely tested in dealing with the Russians. After Stalin's death in 1953, Chinese-Russian relations remained correct and cordial, trade continued, and the Russians gave the Chinese more technical assistance. Russia cooperated with China in railway construction across Outer Mongolia and Sinkiang, supplied the men and materials for China's first Five-Year Plan, aided China's nuclear development, and championed the cause of China at the United Nations. China and Russia represented a communist monolith in 1954 when Khrushchev and Bulganin visited Peking in a spirit of good fellowship. And yet it was the advent of Khrushchev that led to the first signs of trouble. In 1956, speaking to the Twentieth Congress of the Communist Party of the Soviet Union, Khrushchev announced new interpretations of doctrine that were unacceptable to Mao Tse-tung. Besides discounting the necessity of armed struggle and maintaining that war is not inevitable, Khrushchev denounced Stalin and the cult of the individual—to Mao's distress. Stalin today, maybe Mao tomorrow.

When revolutions broke out in Hungary and Poland, the Chinese supported the Russians. Neither China nor Russia wanted anarchy within the communist bloc. But when Khrushchev took over the Chinese policy of peaceful coexistence and applied it to the United States, the Chinese were furious. Coexistence with Asian neutralists was acceptable, but coexistence with the leader of the imperialist camp was not. The Chinese held their tongues until—after the successful orbiting of the satellite Sputnik—the Russians convened an international gathering of Communists in Moscow in 1957. Mao himself attended to argue the views of China. He could trust Chou En-lai in matters of national interests, but not in interpretation of dogma.

The Russians suggested that Lenin should no longer be taken too literally because his teachings were formulated prior to the advent of nuclear power, which invalidated the old belief in the inevitability of war. "Revisionists," whispered the Chinese. "Dogmatists," replied the Russians. In the Chinese view, Russia's spectacular achievements demonstrated that the imperialists were indeed paper tigers and that at last "The East Wind has prevailed over the West Wind." Mao and his cohorts were bellicose in advocating all-out support of wars of national liberation and democratic movements everywhere regardless of imperialist opposition. "What difference if there is a nuclear war, if glorious communist regimes could be established on the debris of dead imperialism?" The Russians pointed out that in any nuclear war there would be no winners, since both communists and imperialists would perish.

This Moscow meeting was perhaps the turning point when, after three years of getting along with the capitalists, China reverted to the old line of revolution and class struggle. In further compromise, Mao could foresee only the obliteration of China's accomplishments and the return of the old second-class position in dealing with the West. When Mao left Moscow, he was reconciled to the continuation of Russian aid, but he was ready to venture into the commune system, the Great Leap Forward, and his own particular brand of socialism.

Mao recoiled from Russia's rejection of Stalin. Stalin today, maybe Mao tomorrow.

The year 1957 was for China a period of agonizing reappraisal of its relations with the United States and Japan. At the Geneva Conference following the Korean War, Chou En-lai took the position that "interference in the internal affairs of Asian nations should be stopped, all foreign military bases in Asia be removed, foreign armed forces stationed in Asian countries be withdrawn, the remilitarization of Japan be prevented, and all economic blockades and restrictions be abolished." He was confronted with the stubborn American policy of strengthening the American military potential in Japan, Korea, Okinawa, Taiwan, and the Philippines; increasing U.S. commitment to Indochina; and creating the Southeast Asia Treaty Organization (SEATO) as the capstone in a defense system to encircle or contain the power of China.

China and the United States descended to the level of confirmed hostility but opened a channel of diplomatic communication short of recognition. The two governments agreed to discuss, first at Geneva and subsequently at Warsaw, the release of Americans held in China and all other matters in dispute. After 1955 China and the United States conducted marathon talks on such topics as the use of force in the Taiwan Straits, lifting trade embargoes, official visits, the possibility of a cultural pact, and the exchange of students, scholars, and journalists. It was not true that during those years the two nations stuck their heads in the sand and ignored each other's existence. They conducted interminable relations but could not reach points of agreement.

Playing a cat-and-mouse game with Japan, China consistently opposed the reactionary Japanese government but uniformly acknowledged the good qualities of the Japanese people. After Japan regained its independence in 1952, China continued to call Japan an American colony and the Japanese government the tool of American imperialism. At the time of the Khrushchev visit to Peking in 1954, both China and Russia declared that the two communist governments stood ready to normalize relations with Japan. China appealed to Japan on the basis of their common "Asian-ness," love of complete independence, and hatred of all militarism, bases, and atomic bombs. China discarded overt relations with Japanese Communists in order to woo Japan's apolitical, conservative businessmen and the left-wing and middle-of-the-road Socialists.

Through 1957 the strategy of accommodation prevailed as China stressed its desire for more trade with Japan, a fishing agreement, and more visits from Japanese unofficial delegations. China blamed the United States for most China–Japan difficulties but intimated that the restoration of normal relations between China and Japan would not require prior rupture of Japan–United States relations or the complete de-recognition of Taiwan by Japan. China admitted the coexistence of states, even powerful neighbors, with different social systems and declared it would deal with any Japanese government, even the conservative government of the Liberal–Democratic–Progressive Party, and would sign a peace treaty with Japan any time Japan might become genuinely "independent, democratic, and free." China offered Japan a nonaggression treaty and proposed a multilateral collective security treaty for the Pacific area to take the place of the China–Russia and the United States–Japan defense systems. Although China seemed disposed to make progress on a negotiable path to peace in 1957, it changed both its disposition and its direction during the decade that followed.

From 1957 to 1967

The resumption of the hard line in foreign affairs paralleled closely the internal class struggle against "the top persons in authority who walked the capitalist road." China abandoned the quest for peaceful coexistence and renewed its consecration to the world revolution. Many Americans accused the Chinese of setting out to dominate the world; the Chinese described their objective as putting an end to capitalist imperialism and feudal oppression. On September 2, 1965, Defense Minister Lin Piao, the newly-designated successor to Mao Tse-tung, summarized the guidelines of China's policy: "The seizure of power by armed force, the settlement of issues by war, is the central task and the highest form of revolution. . . . Whether one dares to wage a tit-for-tat struggle against armed aggression and suppression by the imperialists and their lackeys, whether one dares to fight a people's war against them . . . this is the most effective touchstone for distinguishing genuine from fake revolutionaries." This was a pep talk for Communists overseas, telling them how far they should go in conducting their own revolutions, not a Hitler-like blueprint for Chinese aggression.

China's ability to help and inspire revolutionists throughout the world was curbed by the rift between China and Russia. While Khrushchev was willing to negotiate with capitalists, Mao insisted that all capitalist governments were reactionary and war-mongering and that their influence would have to be destroyed. It was impossible for China and Russia to keep their differences in the family as trade between the two nations dwindled from $2 billion to a few tens of millions per year. In 1960 Russia ended its economic assistance and recalled its technicians from China. A bitter dispute arose over polycentrism—whether the international communist movement should have one center or many centers. Russia refused to accept responsibility for any adventurist decision that China might make in Vietnam, Taiwan, or Algeria. Russia and China became bitter rivals for dominant influence within communist parties throughout the world.

Doctrinal rifts were intensified by clashes of national interest. Russia supported the nuclear test ban treaty, while China rejected it and pursued its program of nuclear development in spite of patent Russian opposition. The schism was widened by boundary disputes, arguments over aid to North Vietnam, and conflict in Outer Mongolia. Demonstrations occurred against Chinese in Moscow and against Russians in Peking. The Russians gave up sponsorship of the campaign to admit the People's Republic of China to the United Nations and turned it over to the Albanians. The language of vituperation in diplomatic exchanges and in the public press degenerated to gutter level.

In 1965 Lin Piao wrote, "The Khrushchev revisionists preach that socialism can be built without a proletariat and without a communist party and they have cast the fundamental tenets of Marxism-Leninism to the four winds. They would divert the oppressed nations from the struggle against the imperialists and sabotage national-democratic revolutions, all in the service of imperialism. They are afraid of becoming involved [in war] with the United States, for then their fond dream of Soviet-American cooperation to dominate the world would be spoiled." In China's view, Russia had sold out to the American imperialists and nothing could be worse.

Between 1957 and 1967 China pursued tough policies to build up the security of its home base. In 1961, following the Russian lead, it negotiated a mutual defense treaty with North Korea. China hardened its line toward Taiwan and intermittently shelled the offshore islands. It drove the Dalai Lama out of Tibet and formally established (in 1965) the long-promised Tibet Autonomous Region.

Relations with India cooled off in 1959 when India gave refuge to the Dalai Lama and some 13,000 Tibetan refugees. China seized the occasion to rectify the China-India frontier, but India was in no mood to negotiate. Jealous of its special influence in the border states of Nepal, Bhutan, and Sikkim, India resented Chinese programs of economic assistance and subversive activities among the hill peoples. Most of all, India objected to China's friendly overtures to Nepal and the projected Chinese construction of a highway from Lhasa to Katmandu, Nepal, gateway to the exposed Indian plains.

The China-India frontier is more than 2,000 miles long, comparable to the border between the United States and Canada. The sectors that China wanted to rectify were as widely separated as Washington, Minnesota, and Maine. Although China maintained that the boundary had never been delimited, India insisted on the legality of documents inherited from the British Empire. In the northwest (Ladakh) the Chinese built outposts and constructed a strategic highway, the highest in the world, from Turkestan into Tibet across disputed territory. China and India accused each other of border raids in the middle sector. In the northeast, where the argument hinged on the legality of the MacMahon line (a line determined by a former British official in India), some 50,000 square miles were at stake. Most of the world's sympathy was with India, but the documents supported some of China's claims.

In 1962 China gave India a military lesson, then pulled its troops back to its prehostilities positions except in Ladakh. China lost all patience with Nehru, who preached neutralism, but moved closer to both the Soviet Union and the United States as a consequence of the border war. After Nehru's death, China stepped up its propaganda warfare against India, and the Peking radio treated Shastri and Madam Gandhi with the same bitterness it had used for Nehru. Trade fell off, friendship disappeared, and the five principles of peaceful coexistence between China and India expired. In the midst of the Cultural Revolution, diplomatic relations were broken off between the two countries.

When India lost China's affection, Pakistan gained. China resented Pakistan's membership in SEATO but realized that most of Pakistan's anticommunism was directed against Russia rather than China. Because Pakistan was Islamic, its friendship was useful to any nation that wished to influence the Arabs in the Middle East. China coveted Pakistan's vote for entry into the United Nations. In the issue that really mattered to Pakistan—Kashmir—China showed itself more understanding of the Pakistani position than any of the other great powers.

In 1963, after the China-India border war, China and Pakistan announced their agreement to settle border disputes and to inaugurate air service between the two countries. Later they exchanged cultural and economic missions, and China came forward with an assistance program to Pakistan. State visits were exchanged as the two countries undertook negotiations for an overall treaty of friendship. China went all out for the Pakistani position on Kashmir, and Pakistan supported China's position on Afro-Asian solidarity conferences and on a general international conference to discuss complete prohibition and thorough destruction of all nuclear weapons. By 1967 China and Pakistan had agreed that nuclear weapons should not be introduced into the Indian Ocean area, and China had given Pakistan all-out support in "her just struggle against the Indian aggressor."

If China was fearful of a two-front war—against the Russians in the north and the Americans from Southeast Asia—during the diplomatic hard times between 1957 and 1967, it made no efforts in the direction of appeasement. Peking was cautious, discreet, but adamant in sustaining its position. The clandestine communist radio contented itself with diatribes against nefarious Western designs in Southeast Asia and gave its support to people's liberation movements that would follow Vietnam. China showed itself again less tolerant toward the governments of the neutrals and was presumably more helpful toward incipient insurgents. It condemned the neutrals for any sympathy toward the United States and applauded them for any evidence of an anti-imperialist, anti-colonial stand. This ambivalence was most noticeable in Burma and Indonesia. China showed its muscles on the borders of Burma only to climax a period of negotiation with a treaty of friendship and peaceful settlement of border disputes. The atmosphere of tolerance and goodwill was ended in 1967 when, as a consequence of over-exuberance during the Cultural Revolution, the Chinese embassy in Rangoon was closed, and the Chinese diplomats were brutally dismissed from the country.

China nearly achieved its greatest victory but actually suffered its worst defeat in Indonesia. China flattered Sukarno's ego but lacked the money to compete against Russia's economic offensive. In spite of racial prejudices against the Chinese, Peking was able to garner tremendous influence with the PKI, the Indonesian communist party. Although Sukarno was not wholeheartedly in the communist camp, China supported him to the hilt for his anti-imperialism. Then Peking was implicated in a communist plot to overthrow the Sukarno regime, and in a counter-coup of September 30 and October 1, 1965, Chinese-Indonesian friendship was drowned in a sea of blood. Ethnic Chinese were slaughtered by the tens of thousands or deported to China. Peking's carefully-nurtured policies toward Sukarno only served to deepen the anti-Chinese feelings of Sukarno's successors. The anti-Chinese pogrom, one of the most ruthless in modern history, brought to an end what some observers believed to be a gigantic Chinese-Indonesian scheme to dominate the entire area between the Pacific and Indian Oceans.

Cambodia was the one country in Southeast Asia that China treated with consistent care. China asked no more than Prince Sihanouk's firm, benevolent neutrality in Vietnam and gave Sihanouk spiritual support in his neighborly political quarrels with South Vietnam, the Philippines, and Thailand. China signed the international agreement at Geneva in 1962 for the neutrality of Laos but gave warning that it would take any measures against the United States in Laos that might be required for China's security. China resumed diplomatic relations with Vietnam and

The United States—the ferocious common enemy of all people.

maintained political observers in the Plain of Jars and in the Pathet Lao country in the northeast. Peking approved neutrality for Laos as the cheapest and most effective way to remove Laos from the umbrella of SEATO. This would checkmate the American program to dominate Laos and provide China with all the opportunity it needed to support and encourage subversive ideas. With the approval of the government in Vientiane, the Chinese built roads from China across northern Laos leading to North Vietnam in one direction and to Thailand in the other. China was not disposed to help the neutralist government of Souvanna Phouma but was ready to help implement the program of the Pathet Lao, the communist party of Laos, if ever it should be accepted by the central government. Peking demanded the ultimate evacuation of American forces from Laos, the dismantling of American bases, and the cessation of all air operations against the highlands and the Ho Chi Minh Trail.

Supporting North Vietnam to the hilt, China promised to remain as close to its ally "as the lips to the teeth." China saw the American advance into Vietnam as preliminary to the invasion of China itself; therefore Vietnam and China were engaged in a common struggle, and China would provide every bit of help that Vietnam wanted as long as a single Vietnamese soldier remained in the field against the Americans. The Chinese did not send volunteers simply because the Vietnamese did not ask for troops. China urged Vietnam to fight until the United States was thoroughly beaten and dismissed offers to negotiate because "peace without victory would be entirely empty."

China felt that its troubles, not only in Vietnam but throughout the world, were due to the hostility of the United States, which it described officially as the chief bulwark of world reaction, the international gendarme, the enemy of the people of the whole world. Lin Piao charged, in 1965, that the United States had stepped into the shoes of German, Japanese, and Italian fascism and was trying to build a great American empire by dominating and enslaving the world. He said, "It is the most rabid aggressor and the most ferocious common enemy of the people of the world [but] if the United States insists on launching a third world war, more hundreds of millions will turn to socialism—the imperialists will then have little room left on the globe, and it is possible the whole structure of imperialism will collapse."

In propaganda to their own people, Peking officials gave very little factual information about the United States. They consistently described the United States as a "paper tiger" in spite of its obvious military

China • 59

strength, and gave the impression that the United States was about to collapse because of its race problems, economic embarrassments, student unrest, "moral depravity," and psychological frustrations resulting from the long unsuccessful war. Chinese masses were reminded constantly of the nearness of war in Vietnam, on the very doorstep of China, and were trained to cope with bombing attacks or possible invasions of Chinese territory. While the words of Chinese leaders indicated scorn for the United States, Chinese policies reflected a deep respect for its power. China continued the discreet diplomatic dialogue with the United States at Warsaw in spite of vituperative press releases from Peking.

China was never willing to isolate itself completely from the capitalist world. It looked to Canada, Australia, Great Britain, France, West Germany, and others for opportunities to encourage trade, attract economic assistance, or counter the influence of the United States or the Soviet Union. In dealing with Canada, China encouraged cultural relations, bought grain, and let it be known that China would welcome the normalization of diplomatic relations. The Chinese bought grain from Australia but disdained political negotiations because of Australia's close tie with the United States, particularly in Vietnam. In the case of Great Britain, China withheld full recognition because of alleged discrimination against Communist Chinese nationals in Hong Kong, British support for Taiwan in the United Nations, and "slavish" British devotion to American leadership in world affairs. China praised France for its cultural brilliance and for its spirit of independence toward the United States. After Peking and Paris exchanged diplomatic recognition in 1964, Peking boasted that the Peking-Paris axis would offset the arrogant combination of Washington-London-Moscow. Ideological differences constituted no handicap in relations between China and West Germany. Chinese-German trade was flourishing in 1966, when West Germany announced, to the consternation of the United States, that it would finance and build a complete steel mill for Communist China.

The overwhelming shadow of the United States continued to cloud relations between China and Japan during this decade. On repeated occasions China suggested that, although the war with Japan was not formally terminated, historic economic and cultural ties between the two countries should be strengthened. A constant exchange of delegations, films, and exhibits took place on the people-to-people level. Chinese Communists joined ideological forces with the Japanese left-wing Socialists in denouncing American imperialism and arguing for "independence, peace, neutrality, democracy, and prosperity" for all the Japanese people.

China called off trade relations with Japan in 1958 but renewed them four years later. Annual trade exceeded $100 million in each direction, but further expansion was limited by the continued Japanese interest in

Taiwan and by pressures on Japan exerted by the United States. Japanese businessmen looked forward to greater access to Chinese markets and raw materials and the establishment of direct air service from Tokyo and Osaka to Peking, Shanghai, and Canton.

In their public statements, the Chinese Communists consistently drew a sharp distinction between the Japanese people and their government, which was blamed for the pro-American, anti-Chinese stance. The Chinese distrusted Japanese leadership in the Asia-Pacific Council in 1966 and interpreted the schemes of the Japanese government to penetrate Southeast Asia as an effort to revive the iniquitous, prewar Greater East Asia Co-Prosperity Sphere, which the Chinese had interpreted as a bold attempt to supplant Western imperialism with Japanese imperialism. The Chinese condemned successive prime ministers of Japan for supporting Taiwan and depriving Peking of its rightful seat in the United Nations. The pervading theme of Chinese propaganda was that the Japanese government fostered militarism and made Japanese militarism the willing tool of the United States, that Japan sought to make itself the arsenal and workshop of Asia, and that its fantastic economic progress was an evil harbinger of military aggressiveness.

On the positive side, China wanted Japan to consider the problem of peace (and reparations) to bring World War II to a formal end. It wanted Japan to divest itself of its close dependence upon the United States, to get rid of the security pact, and to limit its activities in Asia to matters of peaceful economic development. Japan was urged to join China in the general program of a nonaggression pact for the Asia-Pacific region, abolition of foreign military bases, complete prohibition of nuclear weapons and destruction of nuclear stockpiles, a commitment to "no first use" of atomic weapons, declaration of a nuclear-free zone for Asia and the Pacific, and a general international conference on disarmament.

The unique feature of China's foreign relations, 1957-67, was the encouragement of worldwide people's wars as a means of destroying American imperialism. China was active in Latin America until it gave in to the Russians in Castro's Cuba. The Chinese carried the torch of Marxism-Leninism into Africa and the Middle East and tried unsuccessfully to perpetuate a series of Afro-Asian People's Solidarity Conferences. China offered to recognize each new African nation as it was created and made overtures for trade pacts and loans. It undertook a significant economic construction program in Yemen and built the railway connecting Tanzania, Zanzibar, and Zambia. A steady stream of third-world political leaders, journalists, and students were invited to Peking.

China stepped up its emphasis on the third world when the United States escalated the war in Vietnam. On September 2, 1965, Lin Piao applied to the third world Mao Tse-tung's theory of the establishment of rural revolutionary base areas and the encirclement of the cities from the countryside. Lin explained:

> Taking the entire globe, if North America and Western Europe can be called the cities of the world, then Asia, Africa and Latin America constitute the rural area of the world. . . . In a sense, the contemporary world revolution also presents a picture of the encirclement of the cities by the rural areas. In the final analysis, the whole cause of world revolution hinges on the revolutionary struggles of the Asian, African, and Latin American peoples who make up the overwhelming majority of the world's population. The socialist countries should regard it as their international duty to support the people's revolutionary struggles in Asia, Africa, and Latin America.

These were fine words, but they fell flat. Almost anywhere in the underdeveloped world in 1967, Peking stood accused of unwarranted intervention and broken promises. Wherever China tried to influence national policies, it encountered capitalist rivalries. Where it tried to win the endorsement of indigenous communist parties, it suffered from Russian competition. Peking demonstrated no peculiar understanding of local issues and no unusual ability in capturing the leadership of anti-imperialistic national movements. China found itself isolated and distrusted because of its excess revolutionary zeal. It was incumbent upon China's leaders to search for new approaches to problems of foreign relations—at exactly the same time they ordered shifts in the domestic course of the Cultural Revolution.

New Strategies After 1967

Peking has not made the slightest alteration in its foreign policy goals, which have remained constant since the foundation of the People's Republic. Changes in tactics after 1967 did not signify any change of heart, yet China became more flexible in conducting diplomacy and recognized many new countries including Italy, Canada, and Chile. Mao himself hinted of a new era of peaceful coexistence. China exhibited a new warmth toward Bulgaria, Rumania, and Yugoslavia to shake Russia's complacency within the communist bloc. More VIPs visited Peking, and the way of life brightened noticeably in the Chinese capital. Propaganda campaigns were less strident, and many anti-American wall posters disappeared. The culmination came with the invitation to President Nixon to visit Peking and the seating of the delegation of the People's Republic in the United Nations.

Within the Asian ring, Peking softened its position on Taiwan ever so slightly. It would not compromise its claim to full sovereignty over the island but conceded the existence of problems amenable to international discussion. There was no relaxation of control in Tibet, no further reduction of tension along the frontiers of inner Asia, but China made friendly gestures toward Thailand and the Philippines while reaffirming its opposition to their grant of facilities for American forces and bases. Realizing that both Thailand and the Philippines were more anti-Chinese than anti-American, China payed little attention to such insurgency groups as the Patriotic Front in Thailand and the Hukbalahaps in the Philippines. Trade missions were sent to Malaysia and Singapore while preparations were made for full diplomatic recognition. Chinese editorials about the South Seas struck a friendly, sympathetic note. Peking practically ignored U Nu's rebel movement in Burma and patched up its quarrels with Ne Win. With all these friendly gestures, Peking recognized that it could not impose its social and political system on Southeast Asia even if it wanted to.

With regard to Indochina, Peking's attitudes hardened. With the firmness of cold steel, Chou En-lai said repeatedly that he opposed the United States on every front in Indochina. He gave full support to the Pathet Lao, as opposed to the neutralist government of Souvanna Phouma in Vientiane. He gave Prince Sihanouk refuge in Peking and facilitated the establishment there of a Cambodian government in exile. At a conference of all the peoples of Indochina meeting in South China, Chou made clear his endorsement of the fundamental principle that those people should solve their problems without outside interference. His support of North Vietnam was unshakable. He would continue to give all possible help of a military nature, and his only policy at a peace table—in Paris, Geneva, or anywhere else—would be 100 percent backing for North Vietnam and the Provisional Revolutionary Government of the South. He pointed out that it would be useless for the United States to try to drive a wedge between the Chinese and their Vietnamese friends.

After the success of the Tet offensive (1968), when it was clear that America intended to pull out of Vietnam, the Chinese began to worry more about the Russians on the north and less about the Americans on the south. To the Chinese, the Americans were enemies, but the Russians were worse—they were traitors to the communist cause. The example of Russian ruthlessness in Europe led the Chinese to believe that the buildup of a million men in Siberia was a giant fig leaf to cover a preemptive strike against China's embryonic nuclear installations. This explained the frantic air raid precautions in the cities of north China. While Russian and Chinese journalists cursed each other in the official press, diplomats conducted a marathon of fruitless border negotiations in Peking.

The depth of Russian-Chinese antagonism was exposed in verbal skirmishes in the United Nations during the India-Pakistan war of December 1971, when Russia backed India and China (and the United

States) backed Pakistan. The Chinese delegate called the Russians "new tsars who cannot hide their hideous features" and accused them of "social imperialism." The Russian delegate, deploring the gutter language, said, "Such demagoguery and chatter about social imperialism makes it possible for the real imperialists to get away with aggression." The old warning about not having two enemies at once prompted China to reassess the condition of its relations with the United States.

It bears repeating that steps on the part of China toward better relations with the United States did not indicate any abandonment of revolutionary principles or reduction in opposition to American "imperialistic" schemes. China merely changed its tactics to protect its own national interest. It seemed advisable for China to lessen tension with the United States for two reasons: first, to release its energies and assets to concentrate on Russia; and second, to offset the growing rapprochement between the United States and Russia (as seen in the progress of the SALT meetings and the consummation of huge economic deals).

No Chinese leader with any knowledge of relations with the United States had any cause to love President Nixon. On the occasion of the announcement of the Nixon Doctrine in July 1969, Nixon was described in a Peking editorial as a "god of plague and war, who really wants to use Asians to fight Asians." On May 20, 1970, after the American incursion into Cambodia, Mao himself released a bitter blast against the United States and President Nixon. Mao made his usual accusations about "Nixon's fascist atrocities," implying the massacring of peoples in other countries and the slaughtering of blacks and whites in his own country. Mao said the Nixon government was beset with utter chaos at home and extreme isolation abroad and that the United States, "which looks like a huge monster, is in essence a paper tiger now in the throes of its deathbed struggle." In his picturesque way, Mao also said, "U.S. imperialism becomes panic-stricken at the mere rustle of leaves in the wind. . . . The angry roar of demonstrators fills the President with fear." Mao concluded his statement with the customary call to "defeat the U.S. aggressors and all their running dogs." (This is the type of rhetoric that has been fed to the Chinese masses for years and constitutes the raw material for impressions of the United States held by just about every Chinese observer on the line of march from the Peking airport to the Forbidden City.)

Early in 1971 Mao gave vent to a different line of reasoning, not in the public press but to his sophisticated colleagues. He said, "I do not trust the imperialists, but I am willing to talk with them." And again, "I do not expect the U.S. to lay down the butcher knife and become a Buddha, but if the U.S. wishes to be a realist, I shall be a realist too." Mao himself made the decisions to invite the American ping-pong team, journalists, scientists, and others, including the President, to visit China. The invitation to President Nixon was scarcely mentioned in the Chinese press.

The process of decision making in foreign affairs, added to the domestic dilemmas of the Cultural Revolution, may have been the deciding factor in precipitating the cataclysmic change in the attitudes of China's leadership. In July 1971, at the moment of the announcement of the Nixon visit, the Peking press attacked those "with treasonable foreign associations," but gave no hint whether "treasonable" referred to associations with the United States or with the Soviet Union. In August frequent reminders were published that China must maintain a high level of military preparedness. In October verbal tirades were printed against "those who lavish praise on heroes, geniuses, and prophets." The ambiguous phrases might have been aimed at Liu Shao-ch'i, Chou En-lai, Lin Piao, or Mao himself. The matter was clarified later when Mao reappeared in public, Chou received increasing prominence, and Lin Piao was erased as a public figure. Lin, the unbending champion of armed struggle, had opposed any softness toward the United States. It was rumored that he and some of his most noted military colleagues had been purged, killed in an airplane crash in trying to escape from China, or put to death for their part in the alleged plot to kill Mao. At any rate, Peking's public documents in December 1971 were signed by "Mao Tse-tung, Chairman of the Central Committee of the Communist Party of China; Tung Pi-wu, Vice-Chairman of the People's Republic of China; and Chou En-lai, Premier of the State Council of the People's Republic of China." (Tung Pi-wu was the Communist representative on the Chinese delegation at the San Francisco organization conference for the United Nations in 1945.)

The prevailing spirit in Peking was expressed in an essay commemorating the fiftieth anniversary of the founding of the Chinese Communist Party: "The danger of war exists, and since we are prepared for war, we are not afraid. . . . Our task is to do a good job in construction at home and leading the revolution of the proletariat abroad. . . . Our country is still poor and weak but we will push on to greater strength in the decades ahead. . . . We will unite with revolutionary peoples everywhere but we will never act like a super-power. . . . The final destruction of imperialism, revisionism, and reactionaries is not far off, the victory of socialism is near."

"If the U.S. wishes to be a realist, I shall be a realist, too."

一九四九年以來的中美關係

**THE
UNITED
STATES
AND CHINA
SINCE 1949**

CHAPTER FOUR

THE UNITED STATES AND CHINA SINCE 1949

On the China mainland 600 million people are ruled by the Chinese Communist Party. . . . That party came to power by violence and, so far, has ruled by violence.

Secretary of State John Foster Dulles,
June 28, 1957

There is no occasion at the present time to meet Communist China at the summit, but the United States would negotiate with that government or even recognize its regime any time it will serve the interests of the United States.

Secretary of State Dulles, January 16, 1958

Now what do the Chinese Communists want? They don't want just Quemoy and Matsu. They don't just want Formosa. They want the world.

Richard Nixon in debate with John Kennedy, 1958

We simply cannot afford to leave China forever outside the family of nations. . . . The world cannot be safe until China changes . . . thus our aim . . . should be to induce change. . . . Dealing with Red China is something like trying to cope with the more explosive ghetto elements in our own country.

Richard Nixon in *Foreign Affairs*, October 1967

[To an unnamed conservative professor:] You know, Professor, I used to think that way too. But it seems to me that times have changed.

> President Nixon, 1969 (Quoted by Professor
> James C. Thomson, Jr., *Pacific Community*,
> Jiji Press, Tokyo, October 1970)

Premier Chou En-lai has extended an invitation to President Nixon to visit China. . . . President Nixon has accepted the invitation with pleasure.

> Press announcement, July 15, 1971

If China was a rapidly changing society with constantly shifting policies after World War II, so was the United States. Only the issues remained constant. Could the champion of world revolution find an acceptable basis for peaceful coexistence with the leader of the "capitalist-imperialist camp"? Could China tolerate capitalist encirclement—or could the United States feel secure without its bases and military forces in Asia and the Western Pacific? Could the two nations find ways to resolve conflicts over Taiwan, diplomatic recognition, and China's representation in the United Nations? Could China be intimidated by nuclear blackmail or threats of collusion between Russia and the United States? Could China tolerate America's contribution to the economic revival and inherent threat of reawakened militarism in Japan? Could China and the United States find a suitable compromise on their antagonistic proposals for conventional and nuclear disarmament? These basic issues were scarcely touched during almost a quarter-century of unrelieved hostility.

In coping with the bitter China heritage of World War II, every administration from President Truman's to President Nixon's was obliged to operate within constraints imposed by the peculiarities of the American system and the commonly accepted rules for the conduct of international relations. The man in the street may conveniently overlook these constraints, but they can never be neglected by the makers of national policy.

When the People's Republic of China was founded in 1949, contacts between Americans and Chinese were as old as the United States itself, but Americans entertained some ideas about China that made it impossible for Washington to deal with the Communist regime with an open mind. The United States looked upon China as its special ward, and Americans liked to think of the Chinese as exotic, inscrutable Orientals. Americans liked their fellow Christian Chiang K'ai-shek and applauded his stand against the Japanese invaders. Americans did not like any atheistic Communists anywhere. The American public could not accept the fact that the Communists had won the civil war in China, or believe

The United States and China Since 1949

Chronology of American Policy

PRESIDENT TRUMAN

1948   Congress enacts aid to China (Chiang K'ai-shek)

1949   White Paper explains loss of China to Communists, State Department conference on policy toward People's Republic of China

1950   McCarthyism, Korea lead to change in non-involvement policy to active support of Taiwan

1951   MacArthur dismissed, truce talks begin at Panmunjom

1952   Congressional hearings investigate loyalty and security inside the government

PRESIDENT EISENHOWER

1953   Korean armistice, U.S. treaty with Korea

1954   French defeat at Dien Bien Phu, Geneva Conference, SEATO formed, treaty between U.S. government and Taiwan

1955   Congressional resolution on Offshore Islands' defense, U.S. begins ambassadorial-level talks in Geneva with Peking representatives, but Dulles ignores Chou En-lai offer to "discuss differences" at Bundung

1956   U.S.-China differences aired at summit meeting with Russia

1957   U.S. and China fail to agree on issues of trade, travel, and cultural exchange

1958   First hint of potential flexibility in Dulles's policy statements, Dulles-Chiang rule out forceful return to mainland despite Offshore Islands shelling

1959   Concern over China's and U.S.S.R.'s support of Laos and Vietnam

1960   Kennedy-Nixon debates on China policy

PRESIDENT KENNEDY

1961   Aid to Laos and Vietnam takes on military character, policy of containment hardens in Asia

1962   U.S.-China differences sharpen in Indochina and throughout the Third World

1963   Deepening U.S. commitment in Vietnam

PRESIDENT JOHNSON

1964   Tonkin Gulf incident, concern about China policy follows China's atomic explosion

1965   Escalation in Vietnam to halt communist expansion

1966   Senate hearings on China policy

1967   Stress on Vietnam diverts attention from China—then in throes of Cultural Revolution

1968   Tet offensive, Paris negotiations

PRESIDENT NIXON

1969   Nixon Doctrine, further evidence of flexibility as U.S. relaxes trade and travel restrictions, Taiwan Straits patrol reduced, U.S.-China ambassadorial talks in Warsaw

1970   Slight relaxation of China's revolutionary posture, U.S. discreetly explores possibility of U.S.-China summit

1971   Ping-pong diplomacy, announcement of Nixon's planned visit to Peking

that the "rag-tag agrarian reformers" possessed the strength or the quality to remain in power.

The problem for the President—in 1949 as always—was the hard-headed, unsentimental determination of what American national interest required in dealing with China. Responsibility belonged to President Truman alone, not to his advisers, the Secretary of State, the China Lobby, the military-industrial complex, or what Peking called "the ruling classes of Wall Street." Such special interests as airlines and missionary societies could plead their cases; oil and tobacco companies and other traders and shippers might yearn for "the world's greatest market"; but it was up to the President to make the final judgment whether what was "good for General Motors" was also "good for the country."

The President could not rely extensively upon the "experts" for advice on China policy, because the "Asian experts" were hopelessly divided in their counsel, and the "communism experts" knew more about Russia and Eastern Europe than they knew about China. Decisions had to be made within the context of conditions existing in China and in the rest of the world as well. China policy had to be formulated under pressure of domestic politics, diplomatic requirements in Europe and the Americas, and the major preoccupation with Russia and the Cold War.

The size of the budget was a practical limitation upon Washington's options, because a security system proportionate to the government's assessment of the China menace would have necessitated a larger and more expensive military establishment than the voters were willing to pay for. Of more fundamental importance, however, was the continuing uncertainty in trying to define the degree of danger that the new China represented to the United States. Was Communist China the same old China under a new dynasty that would soften with the years? Was it more communist or more Chinese? Could it be trusted? Was it hoping to dominate Asia and ultimately the rest of the world? Was it a tool of Russia? No administration was confident it had found the correct answers to these troublesome questions. Each administration pursued the comfortable tactic of avoiding positive conclusions and taking refuge in popular platitudes.

Between 1949 and 1972 the alternation of Democrats and Republicans made little difference in our dealings with China. The Truman-Acheson-Rusk team dealt just as harshly with Peking as the team of Eisenhower-Nixon-Dulles. The Kennedy-Johnson-Rusk team of the sixties followed in the footsteps of its Democratic predecessors, and the Nixon-Rogers-Kissinger combination of the seventies reflected the precedents established by the Republicans' master practitioner of foreign policy, John Foster Dulles. Toughness was the keynote of China policy. No administration, Democratic or Republican, would take the slightest risk of appearing soft on communism.

Concepts of "right" and "wrong" played little part in determining China policy. In protecting their respective national interests, both China and the United States were right in their own eyes, their allies were "right" and their enemies were "wrong." Anything was right that contributed to national security and the public welfare or reduced any challenge to those objectives. Both China and the United States insisted they were motivated exclusively for the benefit of all mankind. Chinese drew a distinction between the *bad* ruling class government of the United States and the *good* American people, just as Americans differentiated between the *bad* communist regime and the *good* Chinese people. In the final analysis, government and people are the same, because governments represent the people in international affairs, no matter whether officials are designated by the party or chosen by popular election.

As national goals, the Chinese gave highest priority to recognition of their great-power status, the liberation of Taiwan, the elimination of the United States from Asia and the Western Pacific, and support of the world revolution. On these goals the Chinese would not compromise. The Americans attached greatest importance to strengthening their allies in Asia, shoring up nations leaning toward communism, and containing the communist menace. The United States government failed to distinguish between "communist" and "Chinese" and, assuming that both amounted to the same thing, often used one term when it might more precisely have used the other. Under these circumstances, clashes between the United States and China were continuous and unavoidable. The Americans sought solutions in accordance with orderly processes that would preserve international stability. The Chinese did not care how drastically they shook the foundations of a world system based on principles they abhorred.

Tensions occasionally led to the brink of war. Neither the United States nor China shrank away from brush-fire wars, but neither seemed disposed to risk all-out nuclear confrontation. Although both nations claimed their actions were defensive and insisted they wanted to ease international tension, each was reluctant to move too far in the direction of compromise. They seemed unable to get together on their timing. When China declared its preference for peaceful coexistence, the United States was inflexible. When the Americans expressed an interest in the broadening of contacts, the Chinese were unapproachable. Both nations had faults and were guilty of mistakes.

The ordinary differences of diplomatic intercourse were compounded by overtones of emotionalism as both Chinese pride and American pride led to mutual charges of arrogance and racism on an international scale. Passions spilled over into domestic politics. Schisms in the Chinese leadership were deepened by arguments over the United States; McCarthyism within the United States took most of the rationality out of the China debates. The United States and China appeared dangerously close to a collision course until Chou En-lai invited President Nixon to visit Peking. The President's acceptance was merely the latest development in a China policy that had its inception in the administration of President Truman.

Truman-Acheson-Rusk: 1949 to 1953

The People's Republic of China became an American problem on the day it was established, October 1, 1949. Harry S Truman was President of the United States, Dean Acheson was Secretary of State, and Dean Rusk was Assistant Secretary for the Far East. The State Department had just released an official "White Paper" explaining that American economic aid, military assistance, and goodwill had been unequal to the task of preventing the defeat of Chiang K'ai-shek and the Kuomintang by the Communists and Mao Tse-tung. The paper said that the Nationalist government had toppled like a bamboo fence in the wind, because of its own weakness and corruption, and no amount of American help could have propped it up.

President Truman called upon knowledgeable people inside and outside the government, without regard for position or political affiliation, to make an agonizing appraisal of the China situation and to examine the ingredients that must go into the making of an intelligent China policy. To what extent should U.S. policy be directed toward saving China from a totalitarian regime and from being used as an instrument of international communist aggression? Should we assume Russian domination of China and therefore direct our efforts toward preventing the spread of communist domination over other countries in the Far East? Should we continue to support Chiang, or was there any other healthy force within China that we could help to defeat the Communists? Should we recognize China, continue trade with the Chinese, and support their entry into the United Nations? Should we take steps to keep the Communists out of Taiwan? Could we use economic measures to embarrass the Communist regime? Would China be Titoist? Would the fall of China to the Communists trigger a domino reaction in Korea and Southeast Asia? What repercussions could be anticipated in Japan? To what extent could the threat of political upheaval triggered by the communist movement be met by military action and to what extent must it be met by measures of economic and social improvement? How would the communist success in China affect our Point Four (economic aid) program, our collective security arrangements, and our bases? How did it affect our policies toward India, Australia, and New Zealand? How could we best use propaganda as an anticommunist weapon, and how could we win the hearts and minds of thinking Chinese all over the world? Those questions promised a probe that would penetrate to the very depths of the China problem.

While the probe was under way, America sought to disengage itself from the last tentacles of the Chinese civil war. On January 5, 1950, President Truman announced that the United States would not provide military aid or advice to the Nationalist forces on Formosa and would not meddle in Chinese internal affairs. Secretary Acheson declared that our first line of defense in the Western Pacific would pass from Japan and Okinawa to the Philippines, but he omitted any specific reference to Formosa (Taiwan)

Recognition became a political litmus test used to distinguish the true blue American from the pink pro-Communist.

Then the Communist Chinese unceremoniously ousted our official representatives from Peking and seized our property. Our reaction was to refuse diplomatic recognition to the new regime and to use our influence to keep it out of the United Nations. Secretary Acheson stated that we would not recognize China because the government was not in control of the entire country, was not in accord with the will of its own people, and manifested no intention to honor its international obligations. Recognition as an issue became a kind of political litmus test: Those who opposed it were politically wholesome, true-blue "pro-Americans," and those who favored it were politically dubious, pink "pro-Communists."

The effort to establish a new China policy on the basis of reason came to an abrupt halt when Senator McCarthy exploded into the national spotlight with his speech at Wheeling, West Virginia, on February 9, 1950. He referred to "Communists" in the State Department as the architects of a policy that provided China with too little too late and "sold China down the river." According to Senator McCarthy, the presence of Communists on the home front, in addition to spies, dupes, and diplomats in the field, explained why we lost China after twenty years of treason. As an ironic counterpoint to Senator McCarthy's charges, Communist China concluded its treaty of alliance with Soviet Russia on February 14, 1950. It looked indeed as if a communist monolith was forming and China might become a tool of the Russians, a "Slavic Manchukuo." A grain of plausibility lurked in Senator McCarthy's allegation that America's tragic disaster in China was a consequence of communism's international conspiracy. The witch-hunt for scapegoats got under way. Any hope for renewed harmonious relations between the United States and China, or for an injection of restraint into China policy, was entirely illusory at the outbreak of the Korean War.

The "cynical, brutal, and naked aggression" (Mr. Acheson's words) against South Korea occurred on June 25, 1950. Two days later President Truman announced his new policy, which fixed the course of the United States in East and Southeast Asia for the next twenty years. From that moment on, President Truman was as doggedly anticommunist as Senator McCarthy, but in a more gentlemanly manner. He did not share the Senator's fear of Communists in the American government, but he decided that the United States had been kicked around long enough in Asia. He thought that all of the difficulties of the United States in Asia stemmed from a common cause—the expansive power of communism expressed through the military capacity of Russia and the potential strength of an awakened, aggressive China. He saw China as a balloon blown up by Russia and straining at every frontier. The balloon would have to be held in check, deflated, or pricked at some point, such as Korea, Taiwan, or Indochina. It was all one situation, one war —call it what you will—and it called for an unshakable, positive stand on the part of the United States.

On June 27, 1950, President Truman made public his momentous decisions. He ordered American air and naval forces to go to the aid of South Korea. The President decided to rebuild the military might of the United States, to strengthen the American forces in the Philippines, and to take full advantage of the bases available to the United States on the perimeter of China. He accelerated negotiations for a peace treaty with Japan as the first step in making Japan an effective ally, and authorized an extensive military and economic aid program in Southeast Asia to make the nations in that area more resistant to communism.

He also ordered help for the French in Indochina. President Truman was not deterred by any fancied rights or wrongs of imperialism or possible justification the Viet Minh might have had in their civil war. Believing that the interests of the United States were threatened by communism, the President felt that the French fight was also an American fight. The French assured him that they did not need men—only weapons—and with material help they could easily overpower the ungrateful Viet Minh. Thus President Truman began a more active policy in Vietnam as an offshoot of his fundamental anticommunist decision in the Korean War. He did not stumble into war in Vietnam. He made a deliberate choice based on the best advice he could obtain from those in whom he placed the most confidence. His decision may have been ill-advised or counter-productive, but it was neither rash nor blind. President Truman had set the precedents his successors would follow in Indochina.

On the same day, the President turned China policy around 180 degrees by abandoning the attitude of noninterference in China's internal affairs. He used the outbreak of fighting in Korea as the occasion to declare that an attack on the Nationalist Chinese forces on Taiwan would be considered as an attack on the United States. He ordered the 7th Fleet to patrol the Taiwan Straits to prevent attack and sent a military mission to Taiwan to assist in the utilization of forthcoming American aid. A succession of economic measures launched by President Truman brought to Taiwan the highest level of living in Asia outside of Japan. As Taiwan became our ally, the United States became a formidable obstacle between Communist China and the achievement of its primary goal, the liberation of Taiwan.

Peking responded to Washington's challenge by massing troops in Manchuria along the Korean border. Until that time, the United States had identified its enemies in Korea as the Russians and the North Koreans themselves, not the Chinese. As General MacArthur noted the change, he began to think of a wider war and urged that Taiwan should be converted into an unsinkable aircraft carrier as a bastion for American defense in the Western Pacific. President Truman silenced the outspoken general.

The Chinese government then accused the United States of aggression in Taiwan and, on October 1, 1950, warned that China would not stand by idly if the imperialists invaded North Korea. When the forces of the United Nations crossed the 38th parallel at the end of October, Chinese "volunteers" entered the war. The United Nations invited the Chinese to discuss the Korean question, but they refused, saying, "The sincere desire of the Chinese to assist the Koreans against United States aggression is absolutely natural, just, magnanimous, and lawful." For the next six months Americans fought the Chinese in Korea. In February 1951 the United Nations passed a resolution condemning China for participating in aggression. In April General MacArthur was relieved of his various commands for breaking the silence imposed upon him by the commander in chief. Truce talks began in July, but fighting continued while negotiations dragged along wearily.

During the remainder of the Truman administration, China policy was hammered out in the committee rooms of Congress as well as on the battlefields of Korea. The years 1951 and 1952 were an open season for attacks on China specialists, including diplomats, military officers, journalists, and scholars. Charges of disloyalty were based on the assumption that American Foreign Service officers in China were anti-Chiang and therefore procommunist. Senator McCarthy perfected the tactics of character assassination by innuendo and guilt by association. He alleged that a government-academic-journalist axis, spearheaded by a research organization called the Institute of Pacific Relations, was responsible for turning China over to the Communists and for betrayal of the American national interest. The investigation of the Institute of Pacific Relations continued beyond the elections of 1952. The search for a new China policy was embalmed as the questions of 1949 were buried in official files.

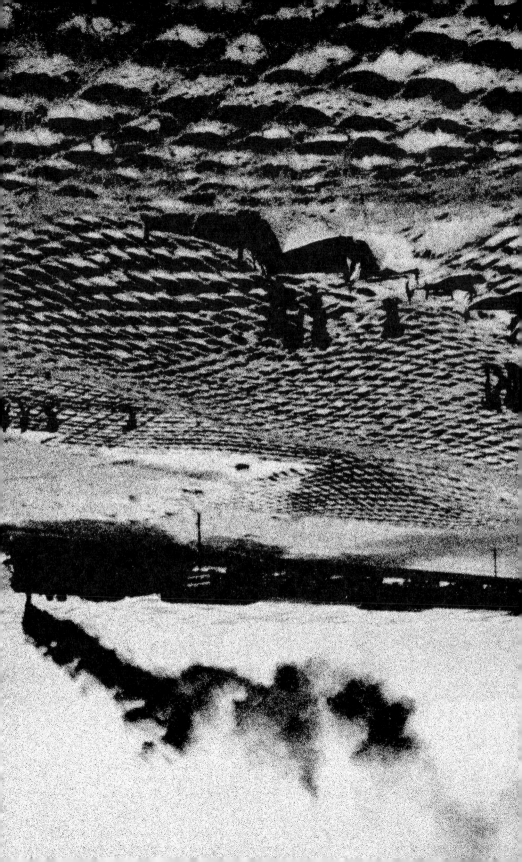

Investigations uncovered very little if any communism, espionage, or treachery, but the morale of the China service was shattered. Some experienced officers were dismissed for "lack of judgment, discretion, and reliability," and others were encouraged to resign. A few were given inconsequential positions in the bureaucracy, and many were transferred out of the Far Eastern area. Instead of concerning itself with *China* as ruled by the communist regime, the State Department was preoccupied with *communism* as interpreted and practiced by its Chinese adherents. Washington came to regard all anticommunist Asian governments as friendly, no matter how reactionary—including Syngman Rhee in Korea, Chiang K'ai-shek in Taiwan, Elpidio Quirino in the Philippines, Phibun Songgram in Thailand, and the Bao Dai emperor in Vietnam. Such socialists, neutralists, and "crypto-communists" as Nehru, Sukarno, Sihanouk, and Lee Kuan-yew of Singapore were treated as the "bad guys."

The U.S. government became less interested in experts with competence in the people, culture, and politics of Asia (particularly China) and more interested in experts in communist theory. Growing increasingly adversary-minded, the administration selected its favorites on the basis of for-me or against-me. Security clearances became infinitely more important for new recruits than intellectual excellence. The ancient, respected British tradition of loyal opposition became anathema, since any evidence of disagreement with prevailing policy gave rise to suspicion and was tantamount to disloyalty. Conformity was more precious than initiative or imagination. If one wished to keep his job, intellectual integrity was possible at any level only for the individual whose convictions agreed with those of his boss. Caution, akin to fear, paralyzed the entire bureaucratic system in its dealings with Eastern Asia.

While McCarthyism played havoc with free thought on China policy, it was dynamite at the polls. Political disaster was the fate of those who were smeared as soft on communism or wrong on China. A smart politician could bolster his claim to almost any office by a fervent denunciation of the communist menace. And no one owed more of his political success to the correct stand on the communist issue than Richard Nixon, who was catapulted into the lofty position of Vice President of the United States.

Eisenhower-Dulles-Nixon: 1953 to 1961

The Eisenhower administration made no sweeping changes in content or methods of China policy but followed in the deep anticommunist grooves of its predecessor. The President ordinarily depended upon his Secretary of State to bear the main burdens of foreign affairs. Half in jest, President Eisenhower once remarked, "If it's in the Bible, and if it's good enough for Foster, it's good enough for me." But in moments of crisis the President demonstrated that he was in firm command. He was at his best in summit conferences with the Russian leaders. When his own hawks pushed him to the brink of war in Indochina in the spring of 1954, President Eisenhower laid down the law: "There will be no hot war in Southeast Asia." Secretary of State John Foster Dulles, a devout Presbyterian layman, gave to anticommunist policies in Europe and Asia the spirit of a religious crusade. He hated communism. To him it was totally evil and should be destroyed, rolled back, or at least contained. Because Russia and China were now acting as an ideological monolith, it was impossible to deal with one without assuming its solidarity with the other.

The crowning achievement of Mr. Dulles's anticommunist crusade was the construction of a formidable-looking mutual security system designed to contain the expansive power of China, or perhaps Chinese communism. The system consisted of a series of treaties with Korea, Japan, the Republic of China, and the seven other nations in the Southeast Asia Treaty Organization (United Kingdom, France, Australia, New Zealand, the Philippines, Thailand, and Pakistan). These treaties were less than treaties of alliance because they represented very limited commitments. They gave the United States the right (but not the obligation) to station forces in other countries and to use their military facilities for the maintenance of peace and international security in the Far East. In the event of an armed attack on any of the parties, the United States promised to meet the common danger in accordance with its constitutional processes. If the territorial integrity, sovereignty, or political independence of any of the parties were threatened in any way other than by armed attack (by insurgency for example), the United States agreed to consult immediately on measures for the common defense. The United States had no positive undertaking to send troops anywhere or to engage in anybody's war. The mutual security system was scarcely enough to provide for the security of the United States and its partners or to guarantee the containment of China or communism. But it was more than a straw man. It served as a psychological deterrent and as a symbol of American intentions. Because the words were flexible, the Secretary of State could put as much meaning into them as he could persuade the American public to support.

When the Eisenhower-Dulles team assumed responsibility for China policy, the Korean truce negotiations were stymied, and Russia was working feverishly to build up the strength of the Chinese homeland during the lull. The armistice was finally concluded on July 27, 1953, but it gave Washington no assurance that aggression had ended. In October the United States signed a treaty with South Korea, the first building block in Mr. Dulles's newly conceived security system. Confident that China had been checked in Korea, the Eisenhower administration turned its attention to Indochina and Taiwan because it feared renewal of Chinese aggression in both areas. The Chinese had made no secret of their help to Ho Chi Minh or their determination to liberate Taiwan. Mr. Dulles, who believed in talking tough, warned China that any renewal of the Korean conflict or a transfer of communist forces into Indochina would mean war against the mainland. The United States was prepared for "massive retaliation."

In spite of the Secretary's bravado, he sensed that the American people shied away from war on the Asian continent, and his European allies were skeptical. France still looked at Vietnam as a civil war that could be won, and England showed little sympathy with American bellicosity. After the French defeat at Dien Bien Phu, Mr. Dulles proclaimed that a Viet Minh victory in Indochina would lead to communist domination of all Southeast Asia. President Eisenhower popularized the theory of the falling dominoes. On April 16, 1954, Vice President Nixon said the United States might have to send troops into Indochina if that was the only alternative to communist domination.

The attitude of the United States at the Geneva Conference of 1954 was symbolized by Mr. Dulles's declining to shake the proffered hand of Chou En-lai. By the Geneva agreements, Vietnam, Cambodia, and Laos were granted their sovereignty; but Vietnam was partitioned, and the question of its unity was to be decided by subsequent elections. South Vietnam withheld its signature because it felt it had no voice in its own fate. The Americans refused to sign the final declaration of the conference but agreed not to disturb it by force. The United States cautioned China against any renewal of aggression.

Then Mr. Dulles negotiated the mutual defense treaty with Taiwan and signed the Southeast Asia Collective Defense Treaty that established SEATO. In South Vietnam the Americans backed Ngo Dinh Diem, supported him in his defiance of the Geneva agreements, and encouraged him to oppose Ho Chi Minh. These unpleasant holding actions were not successful in thwarting the military and diplomatic progress of Communist China. In an off-year election speech in support of a Republican Congressional candidate in 1954, Vice President Nixon voiced the partisan theme that it was the Democrats under Truman who were responsible for the loss of China and the growing crisis in Southeast Asia.

While Chou En-lai preached peaceful coexistence at the Bandung Conference in 1955, the Communist Chinese (in Vice President Nixon's words) "encouraged, invited, and supported insurrection, rebellion, and subversion in every free country in Asia." They were bluntly informed by the United States that, if they persisted in aggression in Southeast Asia, fronts would be opened in Korea and the Formosa Straits with the clear risk of a generalized conflict. The defiant Chinese resorted to force against the offshore islands between mainland China and Taiwan. The Americans replied with the Formosa Resolution authorizing the President to use the armed forces in the offshore islands if, in his judgment, this was the only way to preserve Taiwan. The atmosphere cooled as the United States and China began marathon conversations in Geneva about the release of Americans held in China and other matters in dispute.

In 1956, election year in the United States, the Democrats called ever so softly for a review of China policy. Mr. Dulles gave his view, and therefore the official Republican view, in a famous article in *Life* magazine. He stated that China had taken the United States to the brink of war only to be deterred by determined opposition in Korea and Indochina. If the truce negotiations in Korea had failed, Mr. Dulles wrote, the United States might have attacked Chinese bases in Manchuria and resorted to tactical use of atomic arms. He said also that the President had approved the employment of air power to destroy communist staging areas in China if the Chinese intervened openly in Vietnam. Public approval of tough anticommunist policy was a significant factor in returning the Eisenhower team to Washington.

It was accepted as a matter of creed in Washington that the rule of the Communist Party in China was achieved by violence and maintained by massive forcible repression; that China had taken Tibet by force, defied the United Nations in Korea, supported the communist war in Indochina, and threatened to liberate Taiwan by force; that it fomented communist rebellions in the Philippines and Malaya; and that it was bitterly hateful of the United States. It was therefore considered unwise to make any change in policies of diplomatic recognition, entry into the United Nations, cultural exchange, or relaxation of trade and travel. "However," Mr. Dulles mused, "communist-type despotisms are not so immutable as they sometimes appear."

Nixon accused the Communists of "supporting subversion" . . . a satisfied public sent the Eisenhower team back to Washington.

On January 16, 1958, he told the National Press Club, "There is no occasion at the present time to meet Communist China at the summit, but the United States would negotiate with that government or even recognize its regime any time it will serve the interests of the United States." Later he circulated a memo through his own department: "One day the communist rule in China will pass. By withholding diplomatic recognition from Peiping,* the United States seeks to hasten that passing." Such sentiments as these from John Foster Dulles, the master diplomatist, might well have made a lasting impression on the avid mind of Vice President Nixon.

When Peking unleashed an artillery barrage against the most vulnerable of the offshore islands, Quemoy and Matsu, in September of 1958, the United States was determined to meet force with force. Mr. Nixon said, "The United States could make no greater mistake than appearing to be a paper tiger." Former Secretary Acheson argued, "The United States is drifting toward war with China over issues that are not worth a single American life." When the Communists called off their attack after a fruitless month of shelling, Mr. Dulles was further convinced that American firmness had removed the threat of the use of force from the Taiwan Straits.

With the elections of 1958, a partisan debate on China policy began to assume serious proportions. The Democrats accused the Republicans of "six years of leaderless vacillation in Asia," and the Republicans came back with the time-tested formula that "the defensive, defeatist, fuzzy-headed thinking on the part of the Democrats is the kind of thinking that caused the loss of China and led to the Korean War." The Republicans clearly hated the regime in Peking as sincerely as Peking hated "the ruling classes in Washington." Mr. Dulles pointed out that Peking was transforming China into a great military and industrial power and "their program involves human slavery and cruelty on a scale unprecedented in all world history." In opposing a resolution for Chinese entry into the United Nations in 1959, the American delegate said Communists had kept themselves in power by bloody purges and by liquidation of some 18 million Chinese in nine years. He charged that Communist China had promoted six foreign or civil wars—Korea, Tibet, Indochina, Malaya, and Laos—and concluded, "China's admission to the United Nations would make a mockery of our charter and rob it of all moral authority."

To the end of their administration, the Republicans opposed diplomatic recognition of the Chinese Communist regime on the grounds that it would gravely jeopardize the political, economic, and security interests of the United States. This was no head-in-the-sand policy. Mr. Dulles said, "We deal with the Chinese communist regime wherever it is expedient. We have been in almost constant negotiations with it for particular purposes, at Panmunjom, at the Geneva conference on Indochina, in bilateral negotiations at Geneva and Warsaw." President Ei-

* Peking or "northern capital" is the Communists' name for China's capital city. The Kuomintang on Taiwan still refer to it as Peiping or "northern peace," and officials of the United States government formerly used Peiping in deference to Kuomintang sensibilities.

senhower left office with the public statement, "The United States does not recognize the claim of the warlike and tyrannical communist regime in Peking to speak for all the Chinese people." He declared, "Our position toward China has not changed and will not change as long as Red China continues to do some of the things which we cannot possibly stomach." In one of his last speeches, Mr. Dulles conceded that perhaps some day the communist nations might think more of the welfare of their own people than of foreign aggression, "and when that day comes our relations may be happily dominated by the natural goodwill and friendship that has always prevailed between the peoples of Russia and China and the peoples of the United States." These positions and these sentiments made up the heritage of Mr. Nixon and Mr. Lodge as they campaigned for office in 1960.

Opposition ideas were neither very loud nor very popular. On December 7, 1959, Dean Rusk, now president of the Rockefeller Foundation, issued a report "not proposing United States recognition of the People's Republic of China or its admission to the United Nations" but calling for "reassessment of China's position in the modern world." The report opposed "permitting emotion or differences of ideology to stand in the way of improved relations with the Chinese people." It reflected an urge, particularly on the part of China scholars, to get back to the fundamentals of China issues that had been neglected for more than a decade.

Early in 1960 Senator Jackson called attention to the fact that, in ten short years, the Chinese communist leaders had lifted the country from a prostrate colossus into a giant on the march. Then a group of liberals suggested that the United States should establish direct channels of communication with Peking. The Democratic platform, upon which Kennedy and Johnson stood, contained the following plank:

> We deeply regret that the policies and actions of the government of Communist China have interrupted the generations of friendship between the Chinese and American peoples. We reaffirm our pledge of determined opposition to the present admission of Communist China to the United Nations. . . . Although normal diplomatic relations between our governments are impossible under the present conditions, we shall welcome any evidence that the Chinese Communist government is genuinely prepared to create a new relationship based on respect for international obligations, including the release of American prisoners.

Like the Republicans, the Democrats put the onus for a new relationship on the shoulders of the Chinese. During the Nixon-Kennedy debates, Kennedy took the position that it was "unwise to take the chance of being dragged into war by two islands not strategically defensible."

Nixon replied, "The islands are not important as territory. It is the principle involved. It is in the area of freedom. If we give the islands to the Communists, we start a chain reaction. . . . The surrender of the islands would not lead to peace but to war. Now, what do the Chinese Communists want? They don't want just Quemoy and Matsu. They don't want just Formosa. They want the world. Any surrender only whets their appetite, and the question becomes, 'Where do you stop them?' "

By 1960 new portents appeared in the international skies. It was no longer a bipolar world, half-communist and half-free, if it ever was. The scene of conflict in Southeast Asia assumed new aspects and more menacing proportions. Insurgency was recognized as a more probable cause of war than outright military aggression. Insurgency had local roots as well as outside support, and the United States had overlooked the former in concentrating upon the latter. When flare-ups occurred in Laos in 1959 and 1960, the United States warned all and sundry that it would take a most serious view of any intervention in Laos by the Chinese Communists or Viet Minh armed forces or others in support of the communist Pathet Lao. The newly-elected President of the United States, John F. Kennedy, was not too anxious about the Far East because of his major preoccupation with Cuba and the possibility of peaceful coexistence with Prime Minister Khrushchev.

Kennedy-Johnson-Rusk: 1961 to 1969

On assuming office, President Kennedy accepted the Republican assumption that "the first obstacle to peace is still our relations with the Soviet Union and China." He warned, "We must never be lulled into believing that either power has yielded its ambitions for world domination." The President declared that he had no intention of recognizing China and that it would be extremely difficult to have any kind of normal relations with China as long as they held our prisoners. Secretary Rusk said that he would like to see the reduction of tensions and the participation of China in disarmament talks, but he was unwilling to pay Peiping's price, the abandonment of the government and people of Formosa. Both houses of the newly-elected Congress passed unanimous resolutions against Peking's entry into the United Nations.

Relations with China confronted the new administration in far-flung questions dealing with Laos, Vietnam, Thailand, Cuba, and India. Laos was the first and the worst. Since it was assumed that the Pathet Lao was backed by both China and the Soviet Union, the United States was pleased to avoid more serious trouble by agreeing to the neutralization of Laos at the Geneva Conference of 1961-62. For a short while, to the annoyance of China, the United States stationed a detachment of Marines in Thailand to ward off danger from the direction of Laos.

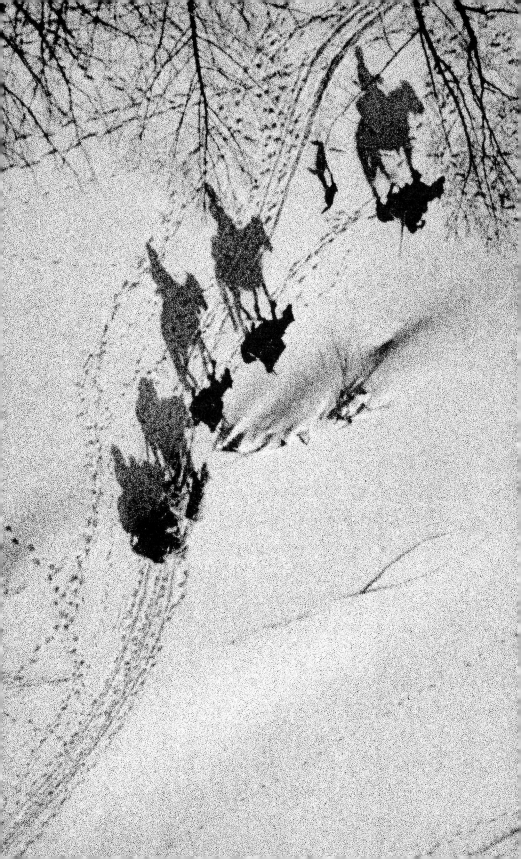

Vietnam, at the outset, seemed comparatively simple to deal with. President Kennedy undertook to help Vietnam "preserve its independence, protect its people against communist assassins, and build a better life." Diem informed Washington that, in spite of American help, his country was in a state of civil war and needed further assistance against outside aggression. He left it to Washington to decide whether "outside" meant Hanoi, Peking, Moscow, or all three. Secretary Rusk said that if Moscow and the other communist capitals would agree to leave these countries alone (Laos, Vietnam, and Thailand), the matter could be solved very quickly. By February 1962 we had 5,000 advisers in Vietnam. Peking commented that the Kennedy administration was "more obsessed and more malignant than Eisenhower in pursuing an aggressive policy which is stubbornly hostile to the Chinese people."

Bitter words were exchanged between Peking and Washington over the Cuban missile crisis and the China-India border clash. Peking, which saw nothing but imperialism in America's relations with Cuba, condemned Khrushchev for "adventurism" in attempting to put his missiles in Cuba and then ridiculed him for "capitulationism" in agreeing to pull them out. Washington expressed shock at the violent, aggressive action of the Chinese Communists against India on the border.

The ideological split within the communist bloc forced the United States to stop making vague generalities about communism and to make a sharp distinction between the policies of Russia and the policies of China. President Kennedy pinpointed China as the source of aggression in Asia. Asked to appraise the power and threat of Communist China (not Chinese communism), he said, "China, with its 700 million people, with a Stalinist internal regime, with its determination for war as a means of bringing about its future success, and with its future potential as a nuclear power, may present in the next decade a potentially more dangerous situation than any we have faced since the end of World War II."

David Brinkley asked President Kennedy if he had any reason to doubt the domino theory, that if South Vietnam falls, the rest of Asia will go behind it. The President replied, "No, I believe it. I believe it. I think the struggle is close enough. China is so large, looms so high just beyond the frontiers, that if South Vietnam went, it would not only give them an improved geographic position for a guerrilla assault on Malaya but would also give the impression that the wave of the future in Southeast Asia was China and the Communists."

The President's last views on China were expressed only a week before his death. He said, "We are not planning on trade with Red China in view of the policy that Red China pursues. If the Red Chinese indicate a desire to live at peace with the United States, with other countries surrounding it, then quite obviously the United States would reappraise its policies. We are not wedded to a policy of hostility to Red China. It seems to me Red China's policies are what create the tension between not only the United States and Red China, but between Red China and India, between Red China and her immediate neighbors to the south, and even between Red China and other communist countries." Neither Mr. Dulles nor Mr. Nixon would have expressed it much differently.

With the advent of President Johnson to the White House on November 22, 1963, increasing frustrations in Vietnam prompted a thorough reexamination of all American policies in Asia. Roger Hilsman of the State Department suggested that we should keep a door open to possibilities of change in dealing with China; but his boss, Secretary Rusk, had very grave concerns about Communist China. He proceeded to list them: "Peiping incited and aggressively supports the aggression in Southeast Asia in violation of the Geneva agreements of 1954 and the Geneva Accords of 1962. . . . Peiping is attempting to extend its tactics of terror and subversion into Africa and Latin America. . . . In other words, Peiping flouts the first condition for peace, leave your neighbors alone." He added as a postscript, "The American people cherish their close and cordial ties with the people of the Chinese mainland. They look forward to the time when it will be possible to renew this historic friendship."

President Johnson gave his views in the spring of 1964: "So long as the Communist Chinese pursue conflict and preach violence, there can be and will be no easing of relationships. . . . It is not we who must reexamine our view of China. It is the Chinese Communists who must reexamine their views of the world." Secretary Rusk said very plainly (June 19) that if aggression did not cease in Southeast Asia, Communist China and North Vietnam risked war with the United States. Admiral Felt, in command of all American forces in Asia, backed him up by saying, "The United States is willing to risk war with Communist China because we believe strongly that it [China] cannot and must not win." Then came the Tonkin Gulf incident and the Congressional resolution authorizing the President to use American forces in Southeast Asia. Tension mounted, but President Johnson took some of the pressure off with his declaration in a campaign speech that he was opposed to involving the United States in war with 700 million Chinese. This announcement was made on the eve of China's first nuclear explosion. The fall of 1964 was given over to the elections, in which the "dovish" President Johnson defeated his more "hawkish" opponent, Senator Goldwater.

When the election was safely over and President Johnson was in office for a new term, he ordered the bombing of North Vietnam. Behind this order, retaliation for the North Vietnamese attack on Americans in the south, was the conviction that the United States had to fight in Vietnam to "halt the communist expansion in Asia." Said Secretary McNamara, who zoomed into the limelight as spokesman for the administration, "Communist China . . . had decided to make Vietnam a test case, but we intended to stand fast." Said President Johnson, "Over this war and all Asia is another reality, the deepening shadow of Communist China."

The escalation of the war in Vietnam brought to the surface all the eddies, whirlpools, and crosscurrents affecting the mainstream of foreign policy. The main issues were the nature of the civil war in South Vietnam, the efficacy of military methods in coping with the local revolutionary situation, the viability of the South Vietnamese government, the wisdom of bombing the north, the degree of responsibility attached to Hanoi as the outside aggressor, and secrecy in United States government operations. At the heart of the matter was the estimate of China's complicity in the Vietnam war and the continued applicability of those familiar interpretations of Communist China that had been in vogue since 1949.

In those days of honest differences of opinion, college and university campuses throughout the country seethed with unrest, with the fervor of teach-ins and demonstrations. It was not a simple alignment of Democrats versus Republicans, liberals versus conservatives, youth versus age, or students versus faculty, because each of these groups and subgroups was divided in its stand on United States policy in Asia. Very few were willing to remain silent while young people were called into service to die, if necessary, for a "cause" that was questionable. Many agreed with the administration and gave wholehearted support to the official line. Some agreed that American objectives in Asia were worthwhile, but argued against the tactics.* Others protested against the whole course of events, expressed moral repugnance to the war in Vietnam and to the entire institution of war, and took violent exception to the men, the establishment, and the system that had permitted American involvement in Southeast Asia. Only the extremes of the spectrum— the lazy, blasé, bored, and apathetic at one end and the hell-raisers at the other—did not bother to find intellectual justification for their attitudes and irresponsible actions. Never was academic freedom more precious or the classroom more exciting than in this period, when the routine of teaching and research was directly and inextricably linked to one of the most vital social issues of our time.

As American involvement in Vietnam proliferated, the Senate Foreign Relations Committee provided an educational forum for a reexamination of the premises upon which United States policy toward China was based. Secretary Rusk opened the March 1966 hearings by expounding

---

* I stood with this group. I joined the late Cecil Thomas, Robert Scalapino, Robert and Pamela Mang, and others in the organization of the National Committee of Cultural Relations with China, dedicated to informing the public about China. I also accepted appointment as an adviser to the Bureau of East Asia and Pacific Affairs in the State Department. I wish to acknowledge my respect and gratitude to the entire "chain of command" from President Johnson and Secretary of State Dean Rusk to Assistant Secretary William Bundy. My opposition to the existing administration's views was well known, but I was given every opportunity to express my convictions.

the administration's point of view. He explained that Peking wanted us out of Asia and wanted neighboring countries to accept subordination to Chinese power. It was just as essential, he said, to contain communist aggression in Asia as it had been to stop Nazi and communist aggression in Europe. China must be stopped in this early phase of its aggressive expansion, just as the Nazis should have been stopped in the 1930s, just as the Soviets were stopped in Greece and Turkey, Persia and Berlin, after the Second World War. If we wanted a better world for our children and grandchildren, we would have to understand that China is the enemy. The United States would help Asians to resist direct or indirect use or threat of force and assist friendly governments to stand up against communist pressures. If Peking were to give up its reliance on force as the best way to settle disputes, show that it was not irrevocably hostile to the United States, and give up its violent strategy of world revolution, we would welcome restoration of the historic ties of friendship between the people of mainland China and ourselves.

Secretary McNamara, who followed Secretary Rusk, was more rigid in his testimony. He believed that the long-range objective of the Chinese Communists was to become dominant in Asia, Africa, and Latin America; that they hoped to create a new alignment, especially in the southern and eastern hemispheres, in which Communist China would be the ideological leader and the most powerful country. There was every reason to conclude that Peiping [sic] was determined to press the conflict in Vietnam at the expense of the Vietnamese people, and we had yet to convince the Chinese Communists that their new drive for world revolution would not succeed. But convince them we must, said Secretary McNamara, or we would have to face them under more disadvantageous conditions than those in Southeast Asia.

A succession of Asia scholars offered contrary points of view. Many argued that we were ill-advised in our militancy and inaccurate in our analysis of Communist China's intentions and capabilities. These scholars insisted that military containment of China was a futile policy, that China was not guilty of military or territorial aggression, that China would fight only if its vital interests were threatened, and that American tough talk was no more frightening to China than China's propaganda was to us. Some advocated containment without isolation—keep the guard up through our ring of bases around the Chinese mainland, but expand contacts with China. Some of the scholars felt that the time had come to negotiate for recognition, to consider a two-China policy for the United Nations, to ease trade restrictions, and to expand opportunities for travel and cultural exchange. Senator Mansfield recommended contacts between Chinese and Americans at the level of the Secretary of State.

While the hearings were in progress, the administration took the initiative in easing restrictions on travel to China for American scholars and tourists. Chinese scholars were invited to visit the United States. In the summer of 1966 President Johnson reaffirmed his hope for reconciliation between the people of mainland China and the world community—including working together in all tasks of arms control, security, and progress—and promised that the United States would persist in its efforts to reduce tensions in the belief that a peaceful mainland China was central to a peaceful Asia. Senator Ted Kennedy suggested a two-China policy for entry into the United Nations, but President Johnson responded, "Not yet." Meeting with the Communist Chinese at Warsaw, the Americans proposed discussion of the normalization of relations and Peking's membership in the United Nations. The proposal met with sharp rebuffs from the Chinese.

Throughout the remainder of the Johnson administration, American enmity in regard to Vietnam was concentrated on Hanoi, but Peking was not entirely forgotten. On October 12, 1967, Secretary Rusk told a news conference that the Vietnam war was a testing ground for Asia's ability to withstand the threat of a billion Chinese armed with nuclear weapons. After the Tet offensive in 1968, after President Johnson's withdrawal from the presidential race and the start of peace negotiations in Paris, China practically disappeared from the headlines. Only Vice President Humphrey, the new Democratic standard-bearer, would not let go of China's complicity in the hostilities of Southeast Asia. "Imagine what kind of a world we would be living in if the sweep of Asian communism should include all of Southeast Asia with its millions of people and its vast resources," Mr. Humphrey said. "Make no mistake about it, Communist China has failed in its attempt to overrun Southeast Asia because we are there resisting aggression. . . . The threat to peace is now in Asia. The threat to our security is in Asia. And we are fighting there not only for the Vietnamese but for ourselves and the future of our country. . . . The fact of the matter is that with the assistance of the United States, SEATO, Southeast Asia and indeed all of Asia has been maintained independent against a powerful force, the Chinese Communists." Candidate Humphrey lost the election, and responsibility for policy in Asia passed back to the Republicans under Richard Nixon.

The Nixon Policy from 1969 to 1972

The personnel of the new team—Secretary Rogers in the State Department and Dr. Kissinger in the White House—was less significant than the fact that President Nixon was its leader. In the grand manner of Franklin D. Roosevelt and John F. Kennedy, Richard M. Nixon took over personal command of foreign policy.

During the Democratic interim between 1961 and 1969, political pressures from both Democrats and Republicans, in Congress and elsewhere, had demanded changes in China policy even to the extent of ending military commitments to Taiwan. A new generation of specialists had appeared on the scene. Uninhibited by McCarthyism, but lacking experience in pre-Communist China, they brought fresh new vigor to the field of Asian studies, and their enthusiasm swelled the tide of protests against the ruts into which American policy had fallen. Although he never admitted that he had been wrong about China, Mr. Nixon showed some signs of brushing away the cobwebs. He could not conceive that perhaps China was a healthy, living organism. He still thought of it as a sick society in need of therapeutic capitalistic medicine, but he would try new ways to treat the patient. He outlined his prescription in the October 1967 issue of *Foreign Affairs*:

> Any American policy toward Asia must come urgently to grips with the reality of China. This does not mean, as many would simplistically have it, rushing to grant recognition to Peking, to admit it to the United Nations and to ply it with offers of trade—all of which would serve to confirm its rulers in their present course. It does mean recognizing the present and potential danger from Communist China, and taking measures designed to meet that danger. . . .
>
> Taking the long view, we simply cannot afford to leave China forever outside the family of nations, there to nurture its fantasies, cherish its hates and threaten its neighbors. There is no place on this small planet for a billion of its potentially most able people to live in angry isolation.
>
> The world cannot be safe until China changes. Thus our aim, to the extent that we can influence events, should be to induce change. The way to do this is to persuade China that it *must* change, that it cannot satisfy its imperial ambitions, and that its own national interest requires a turning away from foreign adventuring and a turning inward toward the solution of its own domestic problems. . . .
>
> Only as the nations of non-Communist Asia become so strong—economically, politically and militarily—that they no longer furnish tempting targets for Chinese aggression, will the leaders in Peking be persuaded to turn their energies inward rather than outward. And that will be the time when the dialogue with mainland China can begin.
>
> For the short run, then, this means a policy of firm restraint, of no reward, of a creative counterpressure designed to persuade Peking that its interests can be served only by accepting the basic rules of international civility. For the long run, it means pulling China back into the world community—but as a great and progressing nation, not as the epicenter of world revolution. . . .
>
> Dealing with Red China is something like trying to cope with the more explosive ghetto elements in our own country. In each case a potentially destructive force has to be curbed; in

each case an outlaw element has to be brought within the law; in each case dialogues have to be opened; in each case aggression has to be restrained while education proceeds; and, not least, in neither case can we afford to let those now self-exiled from society stay exiled forever.*

During his first year in office, President Nixon voiced the Nixon Doctrine based on policy papers submitted to him by the permanent working staff of American specialists on Asia in government service. His main points were that the United States would keep its treaty commitments and would provide a nuclear shield to any nation threatened by communist nuclear blackmail. In instances involving other types of aggression, the United States would furnish military and economic assistance, but it would be up to the nation directly threatened to assume the primary responsibility for providing the manpower for its defense. In other words, "No more Vietnams" and "Asians must defend themselves."

"We move from an era of confrontation to an era of negotiation," the President told the United Nations in the autumn of his first year in office, a year that had seen the first small gestures since 1966 in the direction of liberalization. Travel restrictions to China were further modified; the subsidiaries and affiliates of American companies abroad were permitted to sell nonstrategic materials to China; and American tourists to Hong Kong were allowed to buy goods made in Communist China. Whenever the leaders of Communist China should choose to abandon their self-imposed isolation, President Nixon said, we would be ready to talk with them in the same frank and serious spirit in which we talk with Russia.

In his State of the World message of 1970, the President declared it was certainly in our interests to take steps toward improved practical relations with Peking. (The President no longer used "Peiping" to designate the Chinese capital. He referred to the People's Republic of China, its correct name, rather than "Red China" or "Communist China.") In the months that followed, the United States again reduced limitations on cultural exchanges, travel, and trade. A presidential commission recommended the seating of the PRC in the United Nations, without the expulsion of Taiwan. The General Assembly of the United Nations gave a majority vote to Peking over Taiwan in October 1970. President Nixon, who had once been catalogued as first among the witch-hunters—and had once blasted Dean Acheson as "the head of a cowardly college of communist containment"—had admitted that "times have changed."

In his annual review of foreign policy in 1971, the President said,

---

* "Asia After Viet Nam," by Richard M. Nixon, in *Foreign Affairs*, Oct. 1967, Vol. 46 No. 1: 111–125. Copyright 1967 Council on Foreign Relations, Inc. Reprinted by permission.

"The twenty-two-year-old hostility between ourselves and the People's Republic of China . . . determines our relations with 750 million talented and energetic people. In this decade there will be no more important challenge than that of drawing the People's Republic of China into a constructive relationship with the world community and particularly with the rest of Asia." The President pointed directly to the intense and dangerous USSR-China conflict, rooted in border disputes and aggravated by ideological hostility, power rivalry, and national antagonisms. He said, "A clash between these two is inconsistent with the kind of stable Asian structure we seek. We see no advantage in Chinese-Russian hostility. We do not seek any. We will do nothing to sharpen that conflict, or to encourage it."

Then he went on to say, "We are prepared to establish a dialogue with Peking. We cannot accept its ideological precepts or the notion that Communist China must exercise hegemony over Asia. But neither do we wish to impose upon China an international position that denies its legitimate national interests." He repeated his assurance that our dialogue with Peking could not evolve at the expense of our commitments or of international order. He promised that in the coming year he would carefully examine what further steps might be taken to create broader opportunities for contacts between the Chinese and American peoples. Then he warned against optimism. If the PRC continued to cast the United States in the devil's role and to maintain doctrinaire enmity against us, there was little that could be done to improve the relationship by the United States alone. He concluded, however, "What we can do, we will."

A great thaw took place during the year 1971. President Nixon stopped the 7th Fleet's patrol of the Taiwan Straits, put an end to American (but not Taiwanese) spy flights over China, and acknowledged that the PRC was the legitimate power in control of the mainland. He continued the withdrawal of forces from Vietnam and reduced substantially the number of American military personnel in the rest of Asia. Americans were allowed to travel in China for any purpose (if they could obtain Chinese visas), and exchanges of journalists and students were approved.

The Chinese responded to American overtures with invitations to the American ping-pong team, distinguished scientists, and well-known newspaper and TV correspondents. Mao Tse-tung told the late Edgar Snow that President Nixon could come to Peking if he liked. On July 15, after the secret Kissinger flight to Peking, President Nixon announced that Chou En-lai had invited him to visit China, and he had accepted. The purpose of the meeting was to seek normalization of relations, and exchange views on questions of mutual concern. "Our action will not be at the expense of old friends," said the President. "I believe that all nations will gain from a reduction of tensions between Washington and the PRC." Our friends and allies in Asia were not so sure. In August the

United States announced that it would no longer stand against Peking's entry into the United Nations. On October 25, 1971, Peking was voted in and, in spite of America's will, Taiwan was expelled.

President Nixon arrived in Peking, with hand outstretched, on February 21, 1972. He talked amiably and earnestly for long hours with Chou En-lai and he spent an afternoon in discussion with Mao Tse-tung. He also went sight-seeing, attended ballets, and toasted his hosts at banquets. The President depended upon Dr. Kissinger to carry the main burdens of negotiations during the summit sessions. A joint communiqué was issued on February 27, at the end of the talks with Chou En-lai. It was a modest, restrained expression of good will, but it carried the implication of better relations to come. (The communiqué, as it was published in *The New York Times* on February 28, 1972, is reprinted in the Appendix to this book.)

Two Nations at the Crossroads: 1972

The President was propelled toward normalization of relations with China by many factors including the dollar crisis, frustrations of the war in Vietnam, social unrest at home, the unconscionable cost of our military commitment overseas, and the dazzling prospect that Peking might be a way station on the return to the White House in 1972. It was a long shot that the Peking trip might help in obtaining the release of American prisoners of war.

Some long-unrecognized realities began to emerge in the minds of Americans even as the pendulum of public opinion swung from one extreme to the other—from the jubilation of those who predicted that the President's trip would end "a long night of fear and recrimination" to the condemnation of those who declared, "The Peking visit will take its place with Munich and Yalta in the great trilogy of betrayal." The fact is that we can no longer ignore China or comfort ourselves with platitudes such as "Communism is alien to basic Chinese instincts" and "Sooner or later the Chinese will come to their senses." We can no longer enjoy the smug assumption that we are the "good guys" and the Chinese are the "bad guys."

Some unpleasant facts have begun to shake our complacency. In spite of strains and crises, the Chinese revolution has not collapsed. Whatever the cost, Communist leadership has preserved a facade of national unity and internal stability and seems to have provided a rising standard of living for the burgeoning masses. The Chinese have stood up to Russia on the frontier and to the United States in Korea. Diplomatically, they have won enough friends to vote them into the United Nations. Although they make no apologies for their hard line on world revolution, they have refrained from "adventurism" in Vietnam and elsewhere in Southeast Asia. They have demonstrated their capacity to develop the atomic weapons, nuclear submarines, and medium-range missiles that stand as evidence that China cannot be frightened by dire warnings or threats of chastisement.

The Communists are as confident as their imperial ancestors were of China's superior wisdom and moral correctness. They insist that only the wickedness of reactionary governments has prevented the rest of the world from adopting the thoughts of Chairman Mao. They are taught, "Imperial revisionists and reactionaries cannot harm us with their blockades, embargoes, armed aggression, and subversion from within, which on the contrary encourage us all the more to stand together and to work harder. . . . It is not the Chinese who are isolated but the imperialists, the revisionists, and the reactionaries." The Chinese entered 1972 convinced that the world situation was better than it ever had been for the acceptance of the Chinese point of view on world revolution. In support of this position, they asserted, "The United States as the leader of the imperialist camp is in difficulty. The USSR is in the throes of revisionism, and the peoples of Asia, Africa, and Latin America are ready for Maoist leadership."

It would be a mistake to confuse Mao's revolutionary rhetoric with the Communists' skillful maneuvering and hard-headed planning for the protection of China's national interests. The Communists are masters of Machiavelli. Mao is preeminently Chinese and will keep his place in China's pantheon with the great Chinese emperors, warriors, and scholars of the past and with such modern exponents of Chinese nationalism as Sun Yat-sen and Chiang K'ai-shek. While talking about the world revolution, the Chinese leaders are working actively and pragmatically for security and stability. In foreign affairs they make pronouncements in grandiose and adventuresome tones, but they act cautiously with a keen sense of realities and costs.

The day-to-day diplomatic tactics of Communist China vacillate according to the fluctuations in the prevailing international climate. The Communists say they hate imperialism, but they do not hesitate to make arrangements with imperialists. They make adjustments as required by their own internal quarrels and economic hardships, which means that they may blow hot and cold toward any power—the USSR, Japan, India, or the United States. Like the diplomats of any other nation, the Chinese must respond as well as initiate, and therefore their policies and tactics are affected by the wisdom and determination of the people with whom they deal. With them, as with us, diplomacy is the art of the possible. They cannot adopt an inflexible, irreversible timetable and vow to pursue it, come hell or high water. But because they are patient and accustomed to thinking in terms of protracted conflict, and because they have confidence in the future, they do not mind waiting, no matter how long, for the solution of any diplomatic problem.

Because of its historical record in international relations with Western powers, China puts international prestige high on the list of its priorities. China is not out to make itself the mightiest nation in Asia—

"I have grown old waiting for an enemy to invade . . . but if he comes, we will gobble him a mouthful at a time, or drown him in a sea of people."

only the most important. It dislikes the classification of "super-power," which it considers a term of opprobium. It does not want an Asia ruled by Chinese generals or commissars, but a community of friendly states where China will be looked upon as the model for developing nations, and no political problem will be solved without Chinese participation. China wants implicit recognition of its greatness, and greatness is a matter of culture as well as a matter of guns and the gross national product.

Although China has demonstrated its nuclear capacity and has organized and trained the largest body of armed forces in the world, it is still defense-minded. It is far too weak in modern terms to contemplate armed attack against any major power. China has no armed forces or military bases anywhere beyond its borders. Its military activities at home, including air-raid shelters in all its urban areas, are meant for protection against a possible preemptive strike by Russia, bombardment from the American fleet, or a possible invasion by American forces from the direction of Vietnam or Korea.

"I have grown old waiting for an enemy to invade," said former Foreign Minister Chen Yi, "but if he comes, we will gobble him a mouthful at a time or drown him in a sea of people." Membership in the nuclear club has brought pride to the Chinese people and prestige to the nation, but the chief significance of the achievement is that no one will be able to threaten China with nuclear attack without fear of retaliation. There is no hard evidence that China is less trustworthy with nuclear capability than either the United States or the USSR or that China intends to subject its smaller neighbors to nuclear blackmail.

Although the Chinese Communists have cast an ideological framework for their foreign policies, within that framework they pay the closest attention to the nation's vital interests. Many tactics and strategies that they attribute to the excellence and infallibility of their doctrine, or to the brilliant thoughts of Mao Tse-tung, are deeply rooted in the national interest. Many of their attitudes are more Chinese than communist and would most likely have been adopted by any Chinese government.

The cumulative effect of our own embarrassments in Asia has brought the United States near to the conviction that containment of Communist

China, with or without isolation, has outlived its usefulness. As we have begun to reel under the staggering costs of Vietnam in terms of casualties, money, and social unrest at home, we have been forced to admit that sheer military and economic power are limited as instruments of policy. We have also discovered grave flaws in our security system and programs of assistance.

Our allies, primarily Japan, have pressed us to make an honorable end to hostilities in Indochina and a reevaluation of the dangers we have always presumed to be inherent in communism and Communist China. The disadvantaged nations—such as Indonesia, the Philippines, Thailand, and Malaysia—have sounded a new note of urgency in their appeals for help in their own economic development. Like everyone else, they are eager to find a new path from war to peace. They look to the United States to assume a revised leadership role in the direction of international cooperation. Like the great powers, the people of the smaller nations have rights and responsibilities.

It is entirely too self-centered to think of peaceful coexistence in terms of the United States and China alone, or even in terms of the United States, Russia, and China. The problem is not whether the United States can coexist with the communist powers, or they with us, but whether we can solve our conflicts in such manner as to make living safer for all of us. This responsibility rests as heavily upon the shoulders of China as upon those of the United States. Policymakers of both nations are constrained to use their talents and their resources to seek peace for a whole generation—as President Nixon has repeatedly phrased it, not for ourselves alone but for all mankind.

The relaxation of China's Cultural Revolution and the inauguration of ping-pong diplomacy indicate that, at least temporarily, Mao Tsetung has surrendered his extremism. Has he become a Liu-ist? Has his surrender made a mockery of the entire campaign against "those top persons in authority who walk the capitalist road"? It may be assumed that the recent decisions announced in the name of Mao were made of his own free will, but the China watchers can only guess at Mao's motivation. Perhaps Mao's patriotism has triumphed over his personal de-

---

The U.S. and China seek peace
for a whole generation . . .
for all mankind.

---

sire for revolutionary immortality. He may have felt that he had no alternative but to put the legend of Mao and the cult of the individual at the service of those colleagues with whom he had disagreed so fundamentally. He may have reached the conclusion that China's national interest required the steady hands of the experts rather than the broad vision of the reds. Perhaps power was slipping from Mao's aging grasp, and a multitude of advisers cautioned him that compromise was the only alternative to anarchy or civil war.

Mao must have weighed his decisions carefully in the light of their effect upon those who would come after him. In mid-1971 he disavowed none of his old strategies or tactics. He merely made new options available should they prove advantageous in a new age or under a new directorship. From almost any point of view—personal, political, economic, or foreign policy—Mao and China were at the crossroads on the eve of President Nixon's visit.

Creditable reports from China in the beginning of 1972 indicated that President Nixon could expect a courteous reception, but not a triumphal procession. The visit was likely to be interpreted in China as a modern version of an ancient tributary mission or "an important stage in America's retreat from her military positions in Vietnam and Taiwan." It was generally believed in China that nothing could be resolved with the United States without the settlement of the Taiwan issue. After Taiwan, the less vital problems of Vietnam, Korea, Japan and the withdrawal of all American forces and the abandonment of all overseas bases could be discussed.

Some Chinese were quick to point out that discussion and negotiation did not imply weakness. They said, "Negotiation is struggle. We negotiate and struggle at the same time. That is what we shall do with Mr. Nixon. It is all right if the talks succeed, and it is also all right if they fail. China will never let down its guard or stop preparing for war." In the same vein, other Chinese said, "The Nixon visit cannot harm China. Neither can it in any way lessen China's commitment to the Vietnamese and other revolutionary movements." One Chinese observer wondered whether President Nixon was ready to rebuke his past or alter the role he has played in the Cold War, "or does he still think he is dealing with a savage enemy who has no concern for human ideals?" In his opinion, "Success or failure in the Nixon talks is just a matter of whether Mr. Nixon is ready to repair the damage and injustice which have been done to China."

China's policies toward us are no more mysterious or incomprehensible than ours toward China. Their diplomatic maneuvers fluctuate as they must in the light of their internal turmoil or their difficulties with the rest of the world. When her problems are greatest, China is most uncompromising. When she has confidence in her own stability, she can afford to air her problems with the USSR, her fears of Japan, and her willingness to accept advice and possibly aid from the outside as a spur to her technical development. In such circumstances she can afford to relax in her deepest antagonism to the United States and respond with dignity to any demarche the President might offer. Chinese propaganda is easily turned off or on, and there is no necessary correlation between her words and her deeds. China's attitudes toward us are no more permanent and unchangeable than her attitudes toward any other state. Eager for peace but ready for war, the Chinese can be gracious or tough as the occasion demands.

On our side, we have never been hobbled by a concern for consistency. Maybe approaches should have been made to China in a previous administration, but the time was not ripe and the risk of political suicide was too great. Perhaps President Nixon is the right man, and now is the right time for a return to normalcy. No one anticipates that either Chairman Mao or President Nixon will surrender the minimal requirements for national security. No one expects that Chinese and Americans will immediately become warm friends or that an exchange of toasts will result in a magic era of peace, stability, and economic progress. The leaders of both countries, however, deserve credit to the extent that they show themselves willing to take the first steps on the long, long road to peace and understanding.

The President himself offered the most realistic appraisal of the significance of the Peking visit in the ever-shifting, ever-developing story of the relations between the United States and China. He said he hoped that the meeting might be productive because neither he nor Chou, in public or in private, took the usual, naive, sentimental view that, if we just get to know each other, our differences are going to evaporate. The differences will remain—we have only agreed to discuss them. Later the President added that he expects to make only modest progress in China through steps to expand trade, tourism, and diplomatic contacts.

No one is more aware than the President of the width of the gap caused by ideological differences. Neither the Americans nor the Chinese can hope to change each other. Each must accept the other exactly as he is—without moral self-righteousness—and decide on that basis if it is of mutual interest to make further efforts toward understanding and possibly diplomatic recognition. Both nations stand to gain immeasurably from the reduction of tension. The whole world will benefit if the United States and China, as colleagues rather than as enemies, address themselves to the problems of social and economic development, political stability in Asia, and elimination of the dreadful nightmare of atomic war.

APPENDIX

Text of U.S.-Chinese Communiqué, February 27, 1972

President Richard Nixon of the United States of America visited the People's Republic of China at the invitation of Premier Chou En-lai of the People's Republic of China from Feb. 21 to Feb. 28, 1972. Accompanying the President were Mrs. Nixon, U.S. Secretary of State William Rogers, Assistant to the President Dr. Henry Kissinger, and other American officials.

President Nixon met with Chairman Mao Tse-tung of the Communist party of China on Feb. 21. The two leaders had a serious and frank exchange of views on Sino-U.S. relations and world affairs.

During the visit, extensive, earnest and frank discussions were held between President Nixon and Premier Chou En-lai on the normalization of relations between the United States of America and the People's Republic of China, as well as on other matters of interest to both sides. In addition, Secretary of State William Rogers and Foreign Minister Chi Peng-fei held talks in the same spirit.

President Nixon and his party visited Peking and viewed cultural, industrial and agricultural sites, and they also toured Hangchow and Shanghai where, continuing discussions with Chinese leaders, they viewed similar places of interest.

The leaders of the People's Republic of China and the United States of America found it beneficial to have this opportunity, after so many years without contact, to present candidly to one another their views on a variety of issues. They reviewed the international situation in which important changes and great upheavals are taking place and expounded their respective positions and attitudes.

The U.S. side stated:

Peace in Asia and peace in the world requires efforts both to reduce immediate tensions and to eliminate the basic causes of conflict. The United States will work for a just and secure peace: just, because it fulfills the aspirations of peoples and nations for freedom and progress;

Reprinted with permission from *The New York Times*, Feb. 28, 1972.

secure, because it removes the danger of foreign aggression. The United States supports individual freedom and social progress for all the peoples of the world, free of outside pressure or intervention.

The United States believes that the effort to reduce tensions is served by improving communications between countries that have different ideologies so as to lessen the risks of confrontation through accident, miscalculation or misunderstanding. Countries should treat each other with mutual respect and be willing to compete peacefully, letting performance be the ultimate judge. No country should claim infallibility and each country should be prepared to reexamine its own attitudes for the common good.

The United States stressed that the peoples of Indochina should be allowed to determine their destiny without outside intervention; its constant primary objective has been a negotiated solution; the eight-point proposal put forward by the Republic of Vietnam and the United States on Jan. 27, 1972, represents the basis for the attainment of that objective; in the absence of a negotiated settlement the United States envisages the ultimate withdrawal of all U.S. forces from the region consistent with the aim of self-determination for each country of Indochina.

The United States will maintain its close ties with and support for the Republic of Korea. The United States will support efforts of the Republic of Korea to seek a relaxation of tension and increase communications in the Korean peninsula. The United States places the highest value on its friendly relations with Japan; it will continue to develop the existing close bonds. Consistent with the United Nations Security Council Resolution of Dec. 21, 1971, the United States favors the continuation of the cease-fire between India and Pakistan and the withdrawal of all military forces to within their own territories and to their own sides of the cease-fire line in Jammu and Kashmir; the United States supports the right of the peoples of South Asia to shape their own future in peace, free of military threat, and without having the area become the subject of big-power rivalry.

The Chinese side stated:

Wherever there is oppression, there is resistance. Countries want independence, nations want liberation and the people want revolution —this has become the irresistible trend of history. All nations, big or small, should be equal; big nations should not bully the small and strong nations should not bully the weak. China will never be a superpower and it opposes hegemony and power politics of any kind.

The Chinese side stated that it firmly supports the struggles of all oppressed people and nations for freedom and liberation and that the people of all countries have the right to choose their social systems according to their own wishes and the right to safeguard the independence, sovereignty and territorial integrity of their own countries and oppose foreign aggression, interference, control and subversion. All foreign troops should be withdrawn to their own countries.

The Chinese side expressed its firm support to the peoples of Vietnam, Laos and Cambodia in their efforts for the attainment of their goals and its firm support to the seven-point proposal of the Provisional Revolutionary Government of the Republic of South Vietnam and the elaboration of February this year on the two key problems in the proposal, and to the Joint Declaration of the Summit Conference of the Indochinese Peoples.

It firmly supports the eight-point program for the peaceful unification of Korea put forward by the Government of the Democratic People's Republic of Korea on April 12, 1971, and the stand for the abolition of the "U.N. Commission for the Unification and Rehabilitation of Korea." It firmly opposes the revival and outward expansion of Japanese militarism and firmly supports the Japanese people's desire to build an independent, democratic, peaceful and neutral Japan. It firmly maintains that India and Pakistan should, in accordance with the United Nations resolutions on the India-Pakistan question, immediately withdraw all their forces to their respective territories and to their own sides of the cease-fire line in Jammu and Kashmir and firmly supports the Pakistan Government and people in their struggle to preserve their independence and sovereignty and the people of Jammu and Kashmir in their struggle for the right of self-determination.

There are essential differences between China and the United States in their social systems and foreign policies. However, the two sides agreed that countries, regardless of their social systems, should conduct their relations on the principles of respect for the sovereignty and territorial integrity of all states, nonaggression against other states, noninterference in the internal affairs of other states, equality and mutual benefit, and peaceful coexistence. International disputes should be settled on this basis, without resorting to the use or threat of force. The United States and the People's Republic of China are prepared to apply these principles to their mutual relations.

With these principles of international relations in mind the two sides stated that:

¶Progress toward the normalization of relations between China and the United States is in the interests of all countries.

¶Both wish to reduce the danger of international military conflict.

¶Neither should seek hegemony in the Asia-Pacific region and each is opposed to the efforts by any other country or group of countries to establish such hegemony; and

¶Neither is prepared to negotiate on behalf of any third party or to enter into agreements or understandings with the other directed at other states.

Both sides are of the view that it would be against the interests of the peoples of the world for any major country to collude with another against other countries, or for major countries to divide up the world into spheres of interest.

The sides reviewed the long-standing serious disputes between China and the United States.

The Chinese side reaffirmed its position: The Taiwan question is the crucial question obstructing the normalization of relations between China and the United States; the Government of the People's Republic of China is the sole legal government of China; Taiwan is a province of China which has long been returned to the motherland; the liberation of Taiwan is China's internal affair in which no other country has the right to interfere; and all U.S. forces and military installations must be withdrawn from Taiwan. The Chinese government firmly opposes any activities which aim at the creation of "one China, one Taiwan," "one China, two governments," "two Chinas" and "Independent Taiwan" or advocate that "the status of Taiwan remains to be determined."

The U.S. side declared: The United States acknowledges that all Chinese on either side of the Taiwan Strait maintain there is but one China and that Taiwan is a part of China. The United States Government does not challenge that position. It reaffirms its interest in a peaceful settlement of the Taiwan question by the Chinese themselves. With this prospect in mind, it affirms the ultimate objective of the withdrawal of all U.S. forces and military installations from Taiwan. In the meantime, it will progressively reduce its forces and military installations on Taiwan as the tension in the area diminishes.

The two sides agreed that it is desirable to broaden the understanding between the two peoples. To this end, they discussed specific areas in such fields as science, technology, culture, sports and journalism, in which people-to-people contacts and exchanges would be mutually beneficial. Each side undertakes to facilitate the further development of such contacts and exchanges.

Both sides view bilateral trade as another area from which mutual benefits can be derived, and agree that economic relations based on equality and mutual benefit are in the interest of the peoples of the two countries. They agree to facilitate the progressive development of trade between their two countries.

The two sides agree that they will stay in contact through various channels, including the sending of a senior U.S. representative to Peking from time to time for concrete consultations to further the normalization of relations between the two countries and continue to exchange views on issues of common interest.

The two sides expressed the hope that the gains achieved during this visit would open up new prospects for the relations between the two countries. They believe that the normalization of relations between the two countries is not only in the interest of the Chinese and American peoples but also contributes to the relaxation of tension in Asia and the world.

President Nixon, Mrs. Nixon and the American party express their appreciation for the gracious hospitality shown them by the government and people of the People's Republic of China.

BIBLIOGRAPHY

In preparing this bibliography, Dr. Buss has marked with an * those sources he finds "especially interesting and popularly written." Entries he considers "particularly valuable for their research contribution" he has marked with a §.

This bibliography is selected for interest, availability, reliability, and usefulness. Many of the books listed have excellent study guides. I have found the following to be indispensable: the *Bibliography of Asian Studies*, published annually by the *Journal of Asian Studies* (University of Michigan), and Charles O. Hucker, *China, A Critical Bibliography* (University of Arizona). The periodicals most useful to me are: *The Journal of Asian Studies; Asian Survey* (University of California, monthly); *China Quarterly* (Research Publications, Victoria Hall, East Greenwich, London S.E. 10); *Far East Economic Review* (World Subscription Service, P.O. Box 160, Hong Kong, weekly); *Peking Review* (Peking 37, People's Republic of China, weekly); and *Foreign Affairs* (Council on Foreign Relations, 58 East 68th Street, New York, quarterly). I rely on *The New York Times* primarily for news reports. Government documents are available from the Government Printing Office, Washington, D.C., and from the Foreign Language Press, Peking, distributed in the U.S. by China Books and Periodicals, 2929-24th Street, San Francisco. As a practical matter I have found the Chinese documents I needed in well-stocked college or university bookstores at or near Stanford. They are probably obtainable at large schools elsewhere, too.

The following general historical surveys, or studies of Chinese civilization, are to be found in almost any public library. If any of the titles are missing in yours, why not recommend them to your local board?

Eberhard, Wolfram. *A History of China.* Berkeley: University of California Press, 1950.

Fitzgerald, Charles Patrick. *China, A Short Cultural History.* New York: F. A. Praeger, 1950.

Goodrich, L. Carrington. *A Short History of the Chinese People.* New York: Harper & Row, 1958.

Groussett, Rene. *The Rise and Splendor of the Chinese Empire.* Berkeley: University of California Press, 1964.

Latourette, Kenneth Scott. *The Chinese: Their History and Culture.* New York: Macmillan, 1964.

§Reischauer, Edwin O. and John K. Fairbank. *East Asia: The Great Tradition.* Boston: Houghton Mifflin, 1960-65.

———, and Albert M. Craig. *East Asia: The Modern Transformation.* Boston: Houghton Mifflin, 1960-65.

Schurmann, Franz and Orville Schell. *The China Reader.* 3 vols. Vol. 1. *Imperial China*, Vol. 2. *Republican China*, Vol. 3. *Communist China.* New York: Random House, 1967.

Four titles of unusual interest because of their illustrations are:

China—Land of Charm and Beauty. Shanghai: The Shanghai People's Fine Arts Publishing House, 1964.

Fitzgerald, C. P. The Horizon History of China. New York: American Heritage, 1969.

Froncek, Thomas (ed.). The Horizon Book of the Arts of China. New York: American Heritage, 1969.

Myrdal, Jan and Gun Kessle. Chinese Journey. New York: Pantheon, 1965.

When looking for material which would be a basis for understanding or criticizing the communist interpretations of modern history, I consulted the following:

Chai, Ch'u and Winberg Chai. The Changing Society of China. New York: New American Library, 1969.

§Fairbank, John K. Tradition and Diplomacy on the China Coast: The Opening of the Treaty Ports, 1842-1854. Boston: Harvard University Press, 1964.

§Feuerwerker, Albert (ed.). History in Communist China. Boston: M.I.T. Press, 1968.

Franke, Wolfgang. China and the West. Columbia, S.C.: University of South Carolina Press, 1967.

Harrison, John A. China Since 1800. New York: Harcourt Brace Jovanovich, 1971.

Hellerman, Leon and Alan Stein. China: Selected Readings on the Middle Kingdom. New York: Washington Square Press, 1971.

§Ho Ping-ti. The Ladder of Success in Imperial China. New York: Columbia University Press, 1962.

Hsü, Immanuel C. Y. The Rise of Modern China. London: Oxford University Press, 1970.

————. Readings in Modern Chinese History. London: Oxford University Press, 1971.

Levenson, Joseph R. Confucian China and its Modern Fate. Berkeley: University of California Press, 1964.

Li Chien-nung. The Political History of China. New York: D. Van Nostrand, 1964.

Li, Dun J. China in Transition: 1917-1911. New York: D. Van Nostrand, 1970.

McAleavy, Henry. The Modern History of China. New York: F. A. Praeger, 1967.

Waley, Arthur. The Opium War Through Chinese Eyes. New York: Macmillan, 1958.

Some of the books have an emphasis on pre-communist revolution in China. These are:

*Belden, Jack. China Shakes the World. New York: Harper & Row, 1949.

§Chow Tse-tsung. The May Fourth Movement: Intellectual Revolution in Modern China. Boston: Harvard University Press, 1964.

*Clubb, O. Edmund. Twentieth Century China. New York: Columbia University Press, 1964.

Franke, Wolfgang. A Century of Chinese Revolution. New York: Harper & Row, 1971.

Meskill, John. The Pattern of Chinese History: Cycles, Development, or Stagnation? Boston: D.C. Heath, 1966.

Moseley, George. *China Since 1911*. New York: Harper & Row, 1970.
*Peck, Graham. *Two Kinds of Time*. Boston: Houghton Mifflin, 1950.
Pelissier, Roger. *Awakening of China, 1793-1949*. New York: G. P. Putnam's Sons, 1967.
Rankin, Mary Backus. *Early Chinese Revolutionaries*. Boston: Harvard University Press, 1971.
Simone, Vera. *China in Revolution: History, Documents, and Analysis*. Greenwich, Conn.: Fawcett, 1968.
Spence, Jonathan D. *To Change China: Western Advisers in China, 1620-1960*. Boston: Little, Brown, 1969.
Tan, Chester. *Chinese Political Thought in the Twentieth Century*. New York: Doubleday, 1971.
*White, Theodore H. and Annalee Jacoby. *Thunder Out of China*. New York: Wm. Sloane, 1946.
§Wright, Mary Clabaugh. *The Last Stand of Chinese Conservatism; The T'ung-chih Restoration, 1862-1874*. Stanford: Stanford University Press, 1957.
§————. *China in Revolution: The First Phase, 1900-1913*. New Haven, Conn.: Yale University Press, 1968.

Chapters Two and Three in this booklet reflect a nationwide effort to understand the events in China during the fifties and sixties. We at Stanford played an active role in research and publication. The Hoover Institution, thanks primarily to its distinguished directors and its indefatigable curators of Chinese source materials (Mary Wright, Eugene Wu, and John Ma) built up one of the finest collections on Communist China anywhere in the world. Stanford is well represented among the following titles, which I consider the most useful in understanding Communist China in its early formative days.

Adams, Ruth. *Contemporary China*. New York: Random House, 1966.
Barnett, A. Doak. *Communist China: The Early Years, 1949-55*. New York: F. A. Praeger, 1964.
Buss, Claude A. *The People's Republic of China*. New York: D. Van Nostrand, 1962.
Ch'en, Jerome. *Mao and the Chinese Revolution*. London: Oxford University Press, 1966.
Crozier, Ralph (ed.). *China's Cultural Legacy and Communism*. New York: F. A. Praeger, 1970.
Devillers, Philippe. *What Mao Really Said*. New York: Schocken, 1971.
*Fitzgerald, C. P. *The Birth of Communist China*. Baltimore: Penguin, 1971.
Goldston, Robert. *The Rise of Red China*. New York: Fawcett, 1971.
Houn, Franklin W. *A Short History of Chinese Communism*. Englewood Cliffs, New Jersey: Prentice-Hall, 1967.
Hudson, G. F. *Fifty Years of Communism: Theory and Practice, 1917-1967*. New York: Basic Books, 1968.
Isaacs, Harold R. *The Tragedy of the Chinese Revolution*. Stanford: Stanford University Press, 1962.
Li, Dun J. *The Road to Communism*. New York: D. Van Nostrand, 1969.
North, Robert C. *Moscow and Chinese Communists*. Stanford: Stanford University Press, 1963.
Rue, John E. *Mao Tse-tung in Opposition, 1927-1935*. Stanford: Stanford University Press, 1966.
Schram, Stuart R. *Mao Tse-tung*. Baltimore: Penguin, 1968.

§Schwartz, Benjamin. *Chinese Communism and the Rise of Mao*. Boston: Harvard University Press, 1961.

Shaw, Bruno (ed.). *The Selected Works of Mao Tse-tung*. New York: Harper & Row, 1970.

Snow, Edgar. *Red Star Over China*. New York: Grove Press, 1961.

Van Slyke, Lyman P. *Enemies and Friends: The United Front in Chinese Communist History*. Stanford: Stanford University Press, 1967.

—— (ed.). *The Chinese Communist Movement: A Report of the United States War Department, July 1945*. Stanford: Stanford University Press, 1968.

*Wilson, Dick. *Anatomy of China: An Introduction to One Quarter of Mankind*. New York: Weybright and Talley, 1968.

Some books have more of a contemporary than an historical flavor. I have made no effort to distinguish those which emphasize China's internal developments and those which deal primarily with foreign relations.

Asia Research Center. *The Great Cultural Revolution in China*. Rutland, Vt.: C. E. Tuttle, 1968.

Barnett, A. Doak. *Communist China and Asia: Challenge to American Policy*. New York: Harper & Row, 1960.

—— (ed.). *Chinese Communist Politics in Action*. Seattle: University of Washington Press, 1969.

Barrymaine, Norman. *The Time Bomb: A Veteran Journalist Assesses Today's China from Inside*. New York: Taplinger, 1971.

Baum, Richard (ed.). *China in Ferment: Perspectives on the Cultural Revolution*. Englewood Cliffs, New Jersey: Prentice-Hall, 1971.

*Bulletin of the Atomic Scientists. *China After the Cultural Revolution*. New York: Random House, 1969.

Chai, Winberg (ed.). *Essential Works of Chinese Communism*. New York: Universe Books, Inc., 1970.

Clubb, O. Edmund. *China & Russia: The Great Game*. New York: Columbia University Press, 1970.

Deutscher, Isaac. *Russia, China, and the West: A Contemporary Chronicle, 1953-1966*. London: Oxford University Press, 1970.

Doolin, Dennis J. *Territorial Claims in the Sino-Soviet Conflict*. Stanford: Hoover Institution, 1955.

——, and Robert North. *The Chinese People's Republic*. Stanford: Hoover Institution, 1966.

*Durdin, Tillman, James Reston and Seymour Topping. *The New York Times Report From Red China*. New York: Avon Books, 1972.

Dutt, V. P. *China and the World*. New York: F. A. Praeger, 1966.

Eckstein, Alexander. *Communist China's Economic Growth and Foreign Trade: Implications for U.S. Policy*. New York: McGraw-Hill, 1966.

Evans, Robert. *Report From Red China*. New York: Bantam, 1962.

Fairbank, John K. *China: The People's Middle Kingdom and the U.S.A.* Boston: Harvard University Press, 1967.

Fitzgerald, C. P. *The Chinese View of Their Place in the World*. London: Oxford University Press, 1966.

Geoffroy-Dechaume, Francois. *China Looks at the World—Reflections for a Dialogue: Eight Letters to T'ang-lin*. New York: Pantheon Books, 1967.

Halperin, Morton H. *China and the Bomb*. New York: F. A. Praeger, 1965.

§Hinton, Harold C. *Communist China in World Politics*. Boston: Houghton Mifflin, 1966.

———. *China's Turbulent Quest*. New York: Macmillan, 1970.

Hinton, William. *Fanshen: A Documentary of Revolution in a Chinese Village*. New York: Monthly Review Press, 1966.

§Ho Ping-ti and Tsou Tang. *China in Crisis*. 2 vols. Chicago: University of Chicago Press, 1968.

Hsieh, Alice Langley. *Communist China's Strategy in the Nuclear Era*. Englewood Cliffs, New Jersey: Prentice-Hall, 1962.

Hsu, Kai-yu. *Chou En-lai: China's Gray Eminence*. New York: Doubleday, 1968.

Huck, Arthur. *The Security of China: Chinese Approaches to Problems of War and Strategy*. New York: Columbia University Press, for the Institute for Strategic Studies, 1970.

Keesing's Research Report. *The Cultural Revolution in China: Its Origins and Course*. New York: C. Scribner, 1967.

§Klein, Donald W. and Anne B. Clark. *Biographic Dictionary of Chinese Communism*. Boston: Harvard University Press, 1970.

Lewis, John Wilson. *Major Doctrines of Communist China*. New York: W. W. Norton, 1964.

———. *Party Leadership and Revolutionary Power in China*. Cambridge, England: Cambridge University Press, 1970.

Li Choh-ming. *Industrial Development in Communist China*. New York: F. A. Praeger, 1964.

Lindbeck, John. *Chinese Management of a Revolutionary Society*. Seattle: University of Washington Press, 1971.

MacFarquhar, Roderick. *China Under Mao: Politics Takes Command*. Boston: M.I.T. Press, 1966.

Mao Tse-tung. *Quotations from Chairman Mao Tse-tung*. San Francisco: China Books and Periodicals, 1970.

*Maxwell, Neville. *India's China War*. New York: Pantheon Books, 1971.

*Myrdal, Jan. *Report from a Chinese Village*. New York: Random House, 1965.

*———, and Gun Kessle. *China: The Revolution Continued*. New York: Pantheon Books, 1971.

North, Robert C. *Chinese Communism*. New York: McGraw-Hill, 1966.

———. *Foreign Relations of China*. Belmont, California: Dickenson, 1969.

Ohja, Ishwer C. *China's Foreign Policy in an Age of Transition*. Beacon, New York: Beacon Press, 1969.

Robinson, Joan. *The Cultural Revolution in China*. Baltimore: Penguin Books, 1969.

§Robinson, Thomas. *The Cultural Revolution in China*. Berkeley: University of California Press, 1971.

§Schurmann, Franz. *Ideology and Organization in Communist China*. Berkeley: University of California Press, 1966.

*Snow, Edgar. *The Other Side of the River: Red China Today*. New York: Random House, 1962.

Van Ness, Peter. *Revolution and Chinese Foreign Policy: Peking's Support for Wars of National Liberation*. Berkeley: University of California Press, 1970.

*Walker, Derek. *Government and Politics of Communist China*. New York: Hillary House, 1971.

Wu Yuan-li. *The Economy of Communist China: An Introduction*. New York: F. A. Praeger, 1963.

———, and H. C. Ling. *As Peking Sees Us: "People's War" in the United States and Communist China's American Policy*. Stanford: Hoover Institution, 1969.

For the problems of the United States in China, primary attention must be drawn to the memoirs of Presidents Truman, Eisenhower and Johnson. This is one of the richest fields in American historiography and it will expand at a bewildering rate after President Nixon's demarche to Peking. No book would be better for a Stanford alumnus to put China in its global perspective than Professor Thomas A. Bailey's *Diplomatic History of the American People* (New York: Appleton-Century-Croft, 1964).

§Acheson, Dean. *Present at the Creation: My Years in the State Department.* New York: W. W. Norton, 1969.

Barnett, A. Doak. *A New U.S. Policy Toward China.* Washington, D.C.: Brookings Institution, 1971.

——, and Edwin O. Reischauer. *The United States and China: The Next Decade.* New York: F. A. Praeger, for the National Committee on United States-China Relations, 1970.

Blum, Robert and A. Doak Barnett. *The United States and China in World Affairs.* New York: McGraw-Hill, 1966.

Burnell, Elaine H. *Asian Dilemma: United States, Japan and China.* Santa Barbara: Center for the Study of Democratic Institutions, 1969.

Campbell, John Franklin. *The Foreign Affairs Fudge Factory.* New York: Basic Books, 1971.

Cohen, Jerome. *Taiwan and American Policy.* New York: F. A. Praeger, 1971.

§*China and U.S. Far East Policy.* Washington, D.C.: Congressional Quarterly Service, 1967.

*Douglass, Bruce and Ross Terrill. *China and Ourselves: Explorations and Revisions by a New Generation.* Beacon, New York: Beacon Press, 1970. (I would also call attention to excellent articles by Mr. Terrill in the *Atlantic Monthly*, November 1971 and January 1972.)

§Fairbank, John K. *The United States and China.* New York: Viking Press, 1968.

*Friedman, Edward and Mark Selden. *America's Asia: Dissenting Essays on Asian-American Relations.* New York: Pantheon Books, 1971.

Hilsman, Roger. *To Move a Nation: The Politics of Foreign Policy in the Administration of John F. Kennedy.* New York: Doubleday, 1967.

Horowitz, David. *From Yalta to Vietnam: American Foreign Policy in the Cold War.* Baltimore: Penguin Books, 1969.

House Foreign Affairs Committee. *Sino-Soviet Conflict.* Washington, D.C.: Government Printing Office, 1965.

§——. *United States Policy Toward Asia.* Washington, D.C.: Government Printing Office, 1966.

Iriye, Akira. *U.S. Policy Toward China.* Boston: Little, Brown, 1968.

——. *Across the Pacific: An Inner History of American-East Asian Relations.* New York: Harcourt, Brace and World, 1967.

Kissinger, Henry A. *The Necessity for Choice: Prospects of American Foreign Policy.* New York: Harper & Row, 1961.

Moorsteen, Richard and Morton Abramowitz. *Remaking China Policy: U.S.-China Relations and Government Decision Making.* Boston: Harvard University Press, 1971.

Nixon, Richard. *United States Foreign Policy for the 1970's: Building For Peace.* New York: Harper & Row, 1971.

O'Connor, Richard. *Pacific Destiny: An Informal History of the U.S. in the Far East.* Boston: Little, Brown, 1969.

Paige, Glenn. *1952: Truman's Decision: The United States Sends Troops to Korea.* New York: Random House, 1970.

Ravenal, Earl C. *Peace with China?* New York: Liveright, 1971.

§Senate Foreign Relations Committee. *U.S. Policy with Respect to Mainland China.* Washington, D.C.: Government Printing Office, 1966.

Steele, A. T. *The American People and China.* New York: McGraw-Hill, 1966.

§Tsou Tang. *America's Failure in China, 1941-50.* Chicago: University of Chicago Press, 1964.

U.S. Department of State. *United States Relations with China.* (China White Paper). Stanford: Stanford University Press, 1967.

§Van Slyke, Lyman P. (ed.). *The White Paper: August 1949.* 2 vols. Stanford: Stanford University Press, 1971.

INDEX

ABOUT THE AUTHOR

His interests first aroused as a visitor to the Washington Limitation of Arms Conference in 1921, Professor Claude A. Buss has spent the past half century as a student of China and the Far East. After completing graduate studies at the University of Pennsylvania, he went to China in 1929 as a Foreign Service Officer, serving as attache for language study at Peking and as Vice-Consul and Diplomatic Secretary at Nanking until 1934. Upon his return to the United States he joined the international relations faculty at the University of Southern California. In 1941, he accepted an appointment as executive assistant to the United States High Commissioner of the Philippine Islands. During World War II he was interned for two years by the Japanese. Following repatriation in 1944, he became director of the San Francisco branch of the Office of War Information. He joined the Department of History at Stanford University in 1946 and remained there—interrupting his work from time to time to accept government assignments—until his retirement in 1969. Professor Buss is the author of *The Far East* (1955), *Southeast Asia and the World Today* (1958), *Asia in the Modern World* (1964), and *Contemporary Southeast Asia* (1970). He is currently Lecturer in History at San Jose State University.